KETO DIET FOR BEGINNERS

The Step By Step Guide For Beginners
To Lose Weight Fast And Live Healthier
With The Ketogenic Diet

ELIZABETH WELLS

 The author wishes to thank 123RF / gbh007 for the image on the cover.

TABLE OF CONTENTS

Free Bonus: The Best Foods To Eat On A Ketogenic Diet..........9

Introduction..........11

Chapter 1: The History and Basics of the Ketogenic Diet..........13

Chapter 2: Health Benefits..........19

Chapter 3: How the Ketogenic Diet Works..........28

Chapter 4: Mistakes and Health Risks..........41

Chapter 5: Ketogenic FAQs..........45

Chapter 6: 30 Day Meal Plan..........53

Chapter 7: Recipes..........66

BREAKFAST RECIPES..........66

Spinach, Feta, and Artichoke Breakfast Bake..........66

Loaded Baked Omelet Muffins..........68

Arugula Salad with Prosciutto, Parmesan and Fried Eggs..........70

Eggs with Scallions and Tomatoes..........72

Broccoli and Cheese Mini Egg Omelets..........73

Onion, Red Pepper and Zucchini Frittata..........75

Veggie Ham Egg and Cheese Bake..........76

Sautéed Collard Greens with Bacon..........78

SALADS AND ENTREES..........79

Guacamole Deviled Eggs..........79

Grilled Tuna Arugula Salad with Lemon Vinaigrette....................81

Chicken with Tomatoes and Rosemary..82

Chicken Salad with Strawberries and Spinach.............................84

Zucchini Carpaccio..86

BLT Lettuce Wraps...87

Bacon Parmesan Spaghetti Squash..88

Pancetta with Brussels Sprouts..90

Cobb Salad..91

Asparagus Egg and Bacon Salad with Dijon Vinaigrette...............93

Tuna Lettuce Wrap With Avocado Yogurt Dressing......................94

Chicken and Cilantro Salad...96

Zesty Shrimp and Avocado Salad..98

Zucchini Rolls..99

LUNCH RECIPES...101

Crab Cauliflower Fried Rice..101

Garlic Cuban Pork..103

Steak Kebabs with Chimichurri...105

Grilled Salmon with Avocado Bruschetta...................................107

Turkey Enchilada Stuffed Poblanos...109

Grilled Steak with Tomatoes, Red Onion and Balsamic.............112

Parmesan Chicken with Broccoli...114

Grilled Garlic Chicken with Vegetables....116

Sheet Pan Shrimp with Broccolini and Tomatoes....118

California Spicy Crab Stuffed Avocado....120

Burger Bites....121

Philly Cheesesteak with Portobello Mushrooms....122

Chicken Pesto Bake....124

Chicken Thighs with Artichoke Hearts and Feta Cheese....125

Grilled Prosciutto Wrapped Asparagus....127

Mini Bell Pepper Loaded Turkey Nachos....128

Enchilada Chicken Rolls....130

Grilled Chicken Bruschetta....132

Cheeseburger Salad....134

Chicken with Bacon and Green Beans....136

Grilled Steak Lettuce Tacos....138

Sausage Stuffed Zucchini with Mozzarella Cheese....140

DINNER RECIPES....142

Grilled Salmon Kebabs....142

Brussels Sprouts with Crumbled Blue Cheese....144

Garlic and Lime Pork Chops....145

Grilled Mediterranean Cedar Plank Salmon....146

Braised Cubed Steak with Peppers and Olives Recipe....148

Chicken with Mushrooms with Garlic White Wine Sauce....149

Coconut Milk Shrimp with Tomatoes and Cilantro....151

Grilled Flank Steak with Chimichurri....153

Chicken with Dijon and Lime....155

Grilled Chicken with Spinach and Melted Mozzarella....156

DESSERTS....158

Flourless Keto Brownies....158

Coconut Chocolate Chip Cookies....160

Keto Pound Cake....162

Cinnamon Pecan Bars....164

Coconut Raspberry Slices....166

Peanut Butter Blocks....168

Conclusion....169

Recipes Index In Alphabetical Order....171

Other Books By Elizabeth Wells....174

Free Bonus

The Best Foods To Eat On A Ketogenic Diet

Discover the best foods to eat on a ketogenic diet. You'll learn the different food groups that you should eat to follow the keto diet correctly and start improving your health right now.

Go to **www.eepurl.com/cUqOlH** to download the guide for free.

Introduction

Congratulations! You have just decided to better your life by purchasing this book. *Keto Diet For Beginners: The Step By Step Guide For Beginners To Lose Weight Fast And Live Healthier With The Ketogenic Diet* will teach you everything you need to know about this high-protein, high fat, and low-carbohydrate diet. After reading this book, you will be well on your way to entering the state known as "ketosis" and jump-starting your new weight loss regimen on the Keto lifestyle.

This book will discuss the basics of Ketogenic Dieting and how it differs from so many other low-carb and high-protein diets out there. Some of the topics will be the history of the Ketogenic Diet, where it began, as well as how it is used today. We will discuss many health benefits of eating this way, such as increased energy levels, digestion issues such as acid reflux, gas, and gallbladder problems, just to name a few.

Once we have learned why this diet is so beneficial to our health, this book will dive into how Ketogenic Dieting works as well as the science behind it. In this book, there will also be a straightforward list of foods that can and cannot be eaten.

Lastly, *Keto Diet For Beginners: The Step By Step Guide For Beginners To Lose Weight Fast And Live Healthier With The Ketogenic Diet* provides a complete 30-day meal plan and all the recipes to make your first month on the Keto Diet easy, including desserts! Yes! You can have dessert on this diet! So what are we waiting for? Let's begin the journey to living the Ketogenic Diet lifestyle!

Chapter 1

The History and Basics of the Ketogenic Diet

What is the Ketogenic Diet? Well, we would have to start with where it began. The Ketogenic Diet dates back to our primitive ancestry, about 500 BC. At that time there was no cultivation of crops, so a high-fat, high-protein diet was all that was available to the hunter-gatherer. It has even been discovered that our great ancestors knew the health benefits of eating this way. However, this diet really got its start in the 1920s, when it was used to treat children with epilepsy.

The reason this diet was used is that the diet forces the body into a state of fasting, which has been shown to decrease the amounts of epileptic episodes in a patient. Why? Here's a brief explanation: by removing carbohydrates from our diet, the body begins to burn fats for energy instead of glucose. Usually, carbohydrates get transformed into glucose, a form of sugar, which is essential for energy and normal brain function. When there are no carbohydrates in the diet, this forces the liver to begin changing fat into fatty acids and ketone bodies. The ketones go into the brain, making it a new source of energy. The goal for the epilepsy patients was to reach a state of ketosis, which is when an elevated level of ketone bodies are in the bloodstream.

Simply put, when you eat food high in carbs, glucose and insulin are produced. Glucose is your body's primary source of energy, and insulin is created to keep your glucose levels down in the bloodstream. Insulin also causes fat to be stored in our body. When your body produces too much of it that is when you gain weight. Today's typical modern diet consists of excessive carbs, (be honest now, who doesn't love Fettuccini Alfredo?). Not to mention lack of exercise, all result in weight gain.

Several scientific trials have shown that low-carb diets are much more successful than low-calorie diets, and result in better long-term results. The reason behind this is because a low-carb high-protein diet is much easier to follow than a calorie counting diet because the rules are much more concise, and therefore easier to stick to. Numerous studies have proven results of people losing more weight and were more likely to stick to a low-carb high-protein diet than one that requires calorie counting.

Understanding the Process

In traditional diet plans, those that are considered "healthy" and "effective," they ask you to cut down fats and consume more carbs. But things are different with Ketogenic diet. In keto diet, you need to restrict carbs and replace them with fats - healthy, good fats - to increase metabolism and make you feel good.

Our bodies are used to consuming carbs as a source of energy. Our bodies feel amazing when they consume carbs. While these carbs may seem good and healthy for us, when the body breaks them down, they turn into glucose. And when we consume more sweets and sugar, that could add issues to our health.

For most people, carbs, as a source of energy, is very effective. However, the body feels hungry even before it consumes the carbs, thus making one feel restless, grumpy, irritated, and hungry again.

This results in people consume more carbs just to get the energy back. And once they feel better, they soon become tired, hungry, and restless again. The extra carbs that are being consumed, instead of being an energy source, become excess, unhealthy body fats.

The keto diet breaks that kind of unhealthy cycle. Unlike the traditional diet plans that rely more on carbs, keto diet will limit your carb intake and rely more on healthy fats. That doesn't mean you can't have carbs anymore. You just need to push your body to go to ketosis.

Ketosis is a normal metabolic process in which our body uses our fats as a source of energy. In normal circumstances, when there are not enough carbs, the body will start to consume body fats. To elaborate, the body will break down the stored fats to get glucose (source of energy derived from carbs) from the triglycerides. Ketosis is a by-product of this process. In the ketosis process, it will release a decent amount of Ketones (acid in our blood, that if in high levels, can poison the body) to break down the fats and turn it into an energy source.

Fats are *really* effective energy source. At first, you will feel tired and restless as your body gets a low level of carbs. But soon, you will feel your energy will start to rise again. The fats that you eat and those that are stored in your body will start to burn while making you feel good, full, and satisfied.

But you may ask yourself is a keto diet really the right choice for me? Well here is a checklist you can go through to see if you are the right candidate for this diet and if you are up to the types of challenges you may face on your journey.

- You have tried every other diet out there with little to no results, or you just were unhappy with it.
- Getting tired after meals or have afternoon crashes.
- You want to simplify your eating habits, grocery shopping, and cooking routines
- You feel like you are always hungry.
- If you have food allergies and finding a diet that helps those seems impossible
- Frequent bloating after eating meals

If you said yes to one or more of these issues, then a ketogenic diet and lifestyle is probably a very good diet choice for you. If you are skeptical about the diet, we advise you to consult a healthcare professional to help you choose what diet plan is best for you.

Now that we know about the science behind ketogenic fasting let's look at the basics of it. The premise can be compared to other similar diets out there that involve high-protein and low-carbs. Take for example the Paleo diet, which is based on the same hunter-gatherer idea, however, high fats are not recommended, and neither are dairy or anything that could be considered "cultivated." Paleo, or Paleolithic, really only allows for basic proteins, nuts, fruits, and berries that could have been "gathered" in Paleolithic times. Then there is the well know Atkins diet, which follows the exact same premise as the keto diet, the only difference is in a keto diet you need to continue to consume protein in moderation to avoid leaving the state of ketosis, whereas in Atkins the need to stay in ketosis is only for a short two week period, known as phase 1.

Ketogenic diet plan has different categories. Each category has their own rules. You can choose what kind of keto diet you want. The categories are:

Keto Type 1: In this standard ketogenic diet plan (SKD), you have to consume moderate protein, low-carb, and high-fat foods.

Keto Type 2: Known as the *Targeted Keto Diet* (TKD), this diet plan will require you to add carbs to your diet during your work out.

Keto Type 3: Also called *Cyclical Keto Diet* (CKD), this is done by five keto days and two days for high-carb foods.

Keto Type 4: Similar to SKD, this keto diet plan requires you to consume high-protein foods in all aspects. This diet plan focuses more on protein.

Of these four keto diet plans, only high-protein keto diet (Keto type 4) and SKD were extensively studied. CKD and TKD are mostly for fitness-enthusiasts since both methods are more advanced.

So, to recap, what is the basic premise of the Ketogenic Diet? To enter a state of ketosis, or fasting. How do we do this? By limiting carbohydrates and forcing our livers to produce fatty acids and ketones as the primary source of energy instead of glucose. But besides losing weight, what other health benefits are there to this diet? We will discuss this in the next chapter.

Chapter 2
Health Benefits

The Ketogenic diet has been shown to have significant health benefits besides the overall goal of weight loss. Several studies have been done in recent years and have shown that the low-carb, high-protein lifestyle does have significant health benefits. With each new discovery, more research is being done in conjunction with the keto diet and its links to diseases such as heart disease, diabetes, neurological disorders, and brain health.

The following is a list of the most common benefits that have been linked to the keto diet and how it has improved them.

Weight Loss, Obesity, and Diabetes

Diabetes: As we discussed earlier, when the body has elevated glucose in the bloodstream which is the natural source of energy, this results in a metabolic disorder or Diabetes.

There are two types of diabetes. Type 1 diabetes is when someone's insulin levels are low, which is what helps reduce the glucose levels in the bloodstream. This is typically an inherited disease. Type I diabetics have to inject insulin to regulate their glucose levels. Type II diabetes is when the body does not produce enough insulin in order for the body to function properly, or, some cells in their body do not correctly use insulin to take sugars from the bloodstream. This type of diabetes is not inherited. It results from lifestyle choices, eating habits, being overweight, and lack of exercise. It can be managed with proper dieting, lifestyle changes, and medication. A low-carbohydrate ketogenic diet has shown to reduce Type II diabetes better than when a calorie-restricted diet is followed.

Obesity and Weight Loss:
We discussed in the previous chapter how the keto diet places your body into a fasting state, where it begins to convert fats into energy instead of glucose. This process of breaking down fats requires more energy from your body. This goes without saying that any time you can burn energy and fat, you will see some weight loss. With carbohydrates putting glucose and insulin to your system, the initial reaction will be increased energy, but it can slow you down and make you sluggish once you've come down from that "high." We have all experienced that crushing feeling. Too much glucose has caused your body to go into energy overload and create extra insulin which leads to that unpleasant feeling of tiredness, and sometimes nausea, that people commonly call a "sugar crash."

It is widely known that obesity is rising alarmingly fast. It has been shown to be a large risk factor for numerous cardiovascular and metabolic disorders. Genetics and an inactive lifestyle, combined with a high calorie and carbohydrate diet, leads to excessive weight gain. The ketogenic diet has been proven to help obesity. It is highly effective due to the reduction in appetite because of the high-protein content. Appetite is curbed because proteins help control what are known as "appetite hormones," all resulting in the direct influence of elevated ketone levels in the body.

Prevents Heart Disease

The keto diet can help to prevent heart disease in the sense that by limiting glucose and insulin, you help to lower your blood pressure, lower your triglycerides, and cholesterol.

It may seem odd that eating a higher amount of fat would lower triglycerides, but studies have shown that the consumption of excess carbs like fructose, actually aide in the increase of triglycerides and LDL, your bad cholesterol. Ketogenic dieting has also shown to raise your HDLs, which are your good cholesterol.

Benefits to the Brain

Epilepsy and Seizures: As we learned already, Ketogenic diets were first used in the 1920s to treat epilepsy. It is not known why this diet helped seizures, but researchers now believe it has something to do with stabilization of neurons and increased enzymes which the brain needs to function properly.

Increased brain cognition and memory: Because of the growing attention to this research, consideration has now been given to ketogenic dieting as helpful for Alzheimer's Disease. Further research has revealed the diet helps increase cognition as well as improved memories in adults with brain deteriorating diseases, including all forms of dementia. Ketosis also showed to be helpful in patients with Parkinson's Disease.

A big reason why a ketogenic diet offers benefits to the brain is due to its neuroprotective properties. In order to understand what that means, we have to consider essential fatty acids and their effect on the brain. Doctors have known for years that essential fatty acids such as omega-6 and omega-3 are critical for the brain to function properly. This is because a large amount of our brain is made of fatty acids. The body cannot make its own fatty acids. Therefore, it must be added through diet. A ketogenic diet can be very supportive to this because a large part of the diet is eating a lot of fats.

Eating foods rich in omega-6 and omega-3 like olive oil, coconut oil, avocados, animal fats, fish, eggs, and butter can help nourish the brain and its need for those essential fats. As we already know, when on a ketogenic diet, those ketones that are generated are then used by the brain to create the molecules that carry energy to where it is required for metabolism within cells. As we know now too, ketones are better for the brain than glucose, and this can help the brain be protected from oxidative stress which can affect mental performance and aging of the brain in a negative way.

Having an unbalanced diet can lead to mental fog, lack of clarity, and having a hard time remembering things. This is usually due to glutamate which is a neurotransmitter that can promote stimulation and brain function of one of the main transmitters that reduce stimulation. So anytime you talk, think, or take in information, these two chemicals are involved. When you eat too much glucose and an unhealthy diet, this inhibits these two transmitters, resulting in the fogginess and mental unbalance. By eating a diet that forces ketones to function as the main source of energy, it allows the glutamate and GABA to function properly. Ketones also improve memory by improving the efficiency of cells calls mitochondria, which make the energy for the cells in the body. Ketosis also helps to make new mitochondria which provide energy for the brains energy cells.

Migraines: For a larger amount of dieters, an increase in mental clarity, as well as less frequent and less intense migraines, have often been reported while on the Ketogenic diet. It is believed this is likely related to better brain chemistry which comes from more stabilized blood sugar levels in the blood system creating better enzymes for the brain and thus resulting in less migraines.

Decreasing inflammation

It has been widely known for years that ketogenic dieting has a huge anti-inflammatory impact on the body which can help with a number of different inflammatory diseases. The mechanism behind this may be linked to BHB, one of the central ketones produced from ketogenic dieting. This revelation means that the possibilities for inflammatory diseases such as acne, psoriasis, eczema, arthritis, and IBS, among other diseases involving severe inflammation and pain, have sparked further attention and research.

Acne:

Because of their abnormal effect on hormones, carbohydrates have been suspected of being a large part of why acne develops. When a low-carb diet is eaten that minimizes insulin levels, it reduces inflammation, and from there this results in healthier, clearer skin.

Psoriasis, and Psoriatic Arthritis:
Psoriasis is a skin disease. In normal skin, it takes about 28 to 30 for new skin cells to be produced, and rid itself of the old ones. When one has psoriasis, the body's immune system is oversensitive, and this creates inflammation within the skin and forces the body to make new skin cells faster than normal. These new skin cells then get pressed to the skin's surface in a three to four-day turnaround instead of a normal 28 to 30-day cycle. With this increased rate of new cell development, the body cannot properly dispose of old skin cells, causing thick scaly plaques to form.

Psoriatic Arthritis is a combination of arthritis and psoriasis. The added bonus of Psoriatic Arthritis is you get to experience the itchy scaly plaques of psoriasis along with pain in your joints.

Both these diseases are caused by inflammation. And as we have now learned quite well, by following a ketogenic diet and reducing the causes of inflammation, it can have significant health benefits.

Improving energy levels and sleep
When ketogenic dieting, by day 4 or 5, the majority of people report an increase in their energy levels as well as a general lack of a craving for carbs. The reasoning behind this comes from the stabilizing of insulin levels which naturally result in your body's need for less carbohydrates.

Research on sleep improvements has still been unable to pin down exactly why they improve while on this diet. Studies show that the keto diet does improve sleep through the decrease in REM while creating an increase in slow-wave sleep patterns. While the exact reasoning remains uncertain, it is believed to be due to biochemical shifts that happen in the brain as it uses ketones for energy instead of glucose, as well as other body tissues burning fat

Kidney related issues and Uric Acid

Kidney stones and Gout: It has been shown that the ketogenic diet directly helps kidney related issues such as kidney stones and gout. The reason for this is uric acid. Elevated uric acid levels, combined with elevated levels of calcium, phosphorous, and oxalate have been proven to be the primary cause of kidney stones and gout. These combined with a genetic predisposition, obesity, excessive sugar consumption, and eating or drinking things with elevated purines such as alcohol and certain meats, and dehydration.

A very important note to make is that uric acid levels do elevate at the same time as your ketones go up. If you are a sufferer of gout or kidney stones, it would not be wholly unexpected to possibly have a flare up at this time. However, once you reach the four to six-week mark, despite ketones staying up, uric acid starts to come back down. Also, once you reach the six to eight-week mark on the ketogenic diet, your uric acid levels will come back down to their prior levels, if not even lower.

Gallbladder health and gallstones

Before we go into how the ketogenic diet and how it promotes gallbladder health, it is beneficial to understand that this little organ does and its relation to the liver. The gallbladder is what helps your body process fats in our diet. Because of this, when you eat a diet high in fat, it makes it one of the most valuable organs in your body. The liver is what makes bile that helps to digest the fats. This bile is stored in the gallbladder. When fat and cholesterol are eaten, the gallbladder pumps out the bile, and then the fats are digested.

The majority of people in the United States have gallstones. However, it can take between five and twenty years for any symptoms to manifest. So, if you begin the ketogenic diet and suddenly generate gallstone symptoms, it is likely you already had them, and NOT because of this diet. Gallstones are especially common among women, in particular, those who have been on birth control pills more than a year, or after childbirth. This is because high estrogen levels can cause an increase in the cholesterol levels within the bile, and decreases gallbladder contractions. This can cause gallstones to form.

Cholesterol is what creates gallstones. This happens when it has not been broken down properly in the body. Paradoxically, eating fat will help the body to release bile from the gallbladder. So, when bile is not released regularly, it forms stones

Muscle gain and improvement in endurance

Muscle strength has been specifically linked to BHB, the main ketone created when entering the ketosis state. There have been numerous stories of bodybuilders using the keto diet as a way to gain muscle and strength. Many athletes, in fact, have used the ketogenic diet as a way to significantly improve their mental and physical performance.

In summary, you probably have noticed while reading each health issue, every single health benefit we have discussed all are linked to each other. And all of these diseases have a direct correlation to excess carbohydrates. By removing carbs which lead to glucose, the body begins to function in a healthier way.

As we have now seen thoroughly, following a ketogenic diet and increasing ketone levels within the body will have numerous health benefits. But how does it actually work? How do we get to the state of ketosis? We touched on it earlier, but the next chapter will discuss it in further detail.

Chapter 3
How the Ketogenic Diet Works

As we have now discussed throughout the previous chapters, the ketogenic diet can provide a wide variety of benefits, a better lifestyle, and overall better health. It has proven itself time and again over decades of research. So, now let's get to the fun part. How can YOU start the ketogenic diet? What is needed? What foods can and cannot be eaten? Well, let's begin.

As we have discussed in the previous chapters, the ketogenic diet is based on the premise that by reducing or even eliminating carbohydrates, you force your body to start using fats as energy instead of glucose. This is called ketosis. So, to start, planning will be needed. This means having a diet plan ready and waiting. The faster you want to enter the state of ketosis, it will determine what foods you eat. If you choose a more restrictive meal plan, which would mean keeping all carb intake to a minimum of 15 grams per day, you will enter ketosis much faster. Typically you'll be getting portions of your calories from carbohydrates at 5%, from protein at 35%, and from fats at 65%. However, many people do not like figuring out the percentages of proteins, fats, and carbohydrates, so they do their ketogenic diet by only counting carbs and do not worry about their proteins and fats. , You are considered within the guidelines if your diet stays between 15 and 50 grams of total carbohydrates per day.

You will need to keep your carbohydrates low, and these need to come mostly from vegetables, nuts, and in some version dairy. You cannot eat any refined carbohydrates such as wheat which would include bread, pasta, beans, etc.

You may feel moody, tired, and even slightly nauseated when you first start the ketogenic diet. As your body adjusts to using ketones after carbohydrates for most of your life, it is to be expected. This is called "carb flu." The carb flu typically lasts one to two weeks, there are things you can do to help minimize the symptoms. Drink more water, eat a bit more healthy fats and protein, and consider adding some clean carbohydrates to your diet. Safe choices would be fruit or sweet potatoes.

Once the initial period of transition into ketosis, you will start to experience the mental clarity and increased physical energy. The typical afternoon crashes you experience will no longer bother you, and the improvement in sleep will begin. Your craving will begin to diminish by this point as well.

It is advised to check your ketone levels when you are first beginning the diet. 1 option for doing this include a blood or breathe ketone meter. These meters measure the amount of in your blood or breath. Another option is to test for ketone levels in your urine. You can do this with ketone test strips.

You can find these at any local pharmacy. They are a test strip you dip into your urine, and as it reacts to the ketones in your urine, it changes color. The color it turns indicates what level of ketones you have. Knowing these amounts can be very helpful when you see your levels changing, as it indicates the

Now, what can you eat on a ketogenic diet? We have covered that its low-carb, high-protein, and high fats. But which foods are acceptable and unacceptable? And which will give you the biggest bang for your buck so to speak? So the following is a list of dos and don'ts. The following is an in-depth look at all the foods that can and cannot be eaten, broken down into categories to make it easy to reference if you need to.

MONOUNSATURATED AND SATURATED FATS

- Fatty fish
- Egg
- Butter or ghee
- Nuts and seeds like Peanuts, almonds, macadamia nuts
- Nut butter like peanut butter, Novella, almond butter, etc.
- Olive Oil, Coconut oil, etc.
- Coconut butter
- Cocoa butter

PROTEINS

Moderate protein is a large part of the keto diet, so choosing meats with higher protein content is wise. And if possible choose grass-fed or pasture raised meats. It is recommended that you refrain from buying pre-marinated, or treated meats, as they contain excess sodium, processed ingredients, and sugars.

- Pork: bacon, ground, tenderloin, pork loin, ham, pork chops,
- Eggs: boiled, scrambled, fried and deviled.
- Beef: ground beef, roast, steak, veal, and stews, and the fattier cut, the better.
- Shellfish: clams, mussels, crab, oysters, and lobster.
- Poultry: chicken, turkey, quail, duck. And the darker meats are fattier meats.
- Fish: salmon, mahi-mahi, halibut, catfish, tuna, trout, mackerel, and cod.
- Organ meats: tongue, heart, liver, kidney.
- Goat
- Lamb

CARBOHYDRATES

VEGETABLES (low-carb non-starchy. Leafy greens are always the best choice.)

- Spinach
- Bok Choy
- Kale
- Swiss chard
- Radicchio
- Broccoli
- Onions
- Lettuce
- Brussels sprouts
- Bell peppers
- Asparagus

- Cauliflower
- Cucumber
- Celery
- Zucchini

FRUITS (should be eaten in small amounts due to sugar content. These listed have lower sugar content.)

- Strawberries
- Cherries
- Mulberries
- Blueberries
- Cranberries
- Raspberries

SAUCES AND CONDIMENTS

- High-fat salad dressings with low or no Added sugars
- Yellow mustard
- Horseradish
- Worcestershire sauce
- Sugarless or low sugar Ketchup
- Sugarless Sauerkraut
- Mayonnaise
- Hot sauces

HERBS AND SPICES

Try to stay away from premade spice mixes as they contain many processed ingredients.

- Nutmeg
- Thyme

- Lemon or lime juices
- Parsley
- Rosemary
- Cumin
- Cayenne pepper
- Salt and pepper
- Cilantro
- Oregano
- Basil
- Chili powder
- Cinnamon

SUGARS

There really are no sugars on the OK-to-eat list, however, if you MUST help that sweet tooth, here are your best options:

- Xylitol
- Erythritol
- Liquid Stevia
- Monk fruit

DAIRY

Try to stick to high-fat dairy, as the goal is to have a high-fat diet, and dairy can be an Added source of protein as well.

- Cottage cheese
- Cream cheese
- Heavy cream
- Full-fat yogurts
- Mayonnaise
- Sour cream

- Soft cheese: mozzarella, Monterrey jack, brie, and bleu cheese
- Hard cheeses: parmesan, feta, Swiss, and cheddar

Now that we have seen the approved list of foods, what is on the do not eat list? The following is an extensive list of non-keto foods, broken down into categories.

CARBOHYDRATES
- Wheat
- Barley
- Oats
- Rice
- Corn
- Quinoa
- Rye
- Bread
- Cookies
- Crackers
- Chips

BEANS AND LEGUMES
- kidney beans
- black eye peas
- lentils
- pinto beans
- chickpeas
- garbanzo beans
- green peas
- black beans

FRUITS
- Apples

- Bananas
- Oranges
- Pineapple
- Papaya
- Mangos
- Grapes
- Fruit Juice
- Fruit Smoothies
- Fruit Syrups

STARCHY VEGETABLES
- Yams
- Potatoes
- Cherry Tomatoes
- Carrots
- Corn
- Parsnips
- Peas

SUGARS
- Corn Syrup
- Sugar
- Honey
- Syrup
- Cane Sugar
- Agave Nectar

DAIRY
- Milk
- Shredded cheeses
- Reduced fat or nonfat items
- Hot Dogs
- Lunch Meat
- Packaged sausages
- Processed or treated meats

FATS

- Canola Oil
- Soybean oil
- Virgin Olive oil
- Peanut Oil
- Sesame oil
- Corn oil

DRINKS

- Soda
- Diet Soda
- Smoothies
- Coffee with sweetener
- Tea with sweetener
- Sweetened milk products
- Fruit and vegetable juices

CONDIMENTS

- Anything with the non-keto oils
- Contains sugars
- Labeled Low Fat

ALCOHOL

A nice glass of wine sure is nice in the evening after a hard day of work. Or maybe you are a beer drinker. But does it fit into a ketogenic diet? Well, let us discuss some guidelines that can help you through a decision making process on whether to drink or not drink and how to choose which alcoholic beverages are better than others.

When you drink alcohol, the body considers it a toxin and begins to work hard to process that toxin out as quickly as possible. This means sending it to the liver to process it out, and that in turn takes away the liver's new primary function: creating ketones for your diet. So, this means drinking alcohol slows ketone production, and thus your state of ketosis

So, drinking alcohol suddenly looks a lot different once you start a keto diet. Some people have used a drink as their cheat meal. Before you decide whether to drink or not on this diet, here are a few things to consider before pouring that first glass.

Not all alcohol is the same. They all contain ethanol, which is a fermented form of sugar. But the type of sugar in each alcohol determines which drinks are better than others.
Beer comes from water, hops, yeast, and barley. Beer is probably the worst drink for a keto diet because it is made of all those grains and it contains a lot of carbohydrates, which would essentially kill the ketosis state of your body. Some of the other beverages to avoid that are bad are:

- Flavored alcohols
- Cocktails
- Wines (especially sweet wines)
- Beers
- Sugary mixers that contain soda, syrups, or juices

In short, if it tastes sweet, then it probably has a lot of sugar and carbs. Also, because you are on a reduced calorie diet, so any alcohol will be digested and hit your bloodstream faster, which results in possibly a lower tolerance. Honestly, alcohol is empty calories that could run you off track of your diet. It provides calories that have no benefit to your body.

But, if you decide you need to have that glass of wine with your steak dinner, then here is a list of the best alcohols to drink when on a ketogenic diet.
Hard Alcohols are always a better choice because they do not contain as much sugar as the drinks mentioned above.

- Tequila
- Whiskey, scotch, or bourbon.
- Vodka
- Rum
- Brandy
- Gin.
- Cognac

Safe Chasers

- Diet tonic water
- seltzer water
- sugar-free or diet drinks with stevia or erythritol
- sugar-free carbonated water

WINES AND BEERS

While neither of these is the best choices to drink, here is a list of beers and wines that are slightly better choices.

Reds Wines:

- Cabernet
- Merlot
- Pinot Noir

White Wines:

- Sauvignon Blanc
- Pinot Grigio
- Champagne
- Chardonnay
- Riesling

Beers (always choose a light option)

- Miller 64
- Caroni Light
- Miller Light
- Bud Light
- Michelob Light
- Bud Select 55

Alcohol summary, if you are going to drink, then remember to stay away from anything sweet. If you choose to drink, then clear hard alcohols are your best choices.

CHEAT DAYS

After reading these lists, you may now be wondering if you can have a cheat day on a Keto Diet? The answer is no, and yes. It depends on your weight loss goals. If you want to truly kick your ketosis into high gear, then cheat days are absolutely not recommended. However, as you progress and become more familiar with the allowed foods on a keto diet, you may find that a cheat day is not necessary. You will discover yourself indulging in the approved foods and not having the cravings that a cheat day usually helps to alleviate. That being said, if you are just dying to have that cheeseburger or some ice cream, go ahead and do it, because it is easier to give yourself one day to fulfill cravings than a total breakdown and blow the whole diet.

So, now that you know the basics and have seen what you should and should not eat, as well as how to keep your carb intake down and your proteins and fats up, let's talk a little about mistakes and health risks. We will discuss this in the next chapter.

Chapter 4
Mistakes and Health Risks

We have now been over the keto diet extensively and how it can benefit the body and people who suffer from many different health problems. However, there are risks that can happen while on a keto diet. This diet may not be for everyone, especially those who suffer from some health problems we will discuss in moments. It is important you know that staying on the ketogenic diet long-term can have adverse consequences to your health. Always consult your physician before starting such a drastic diet which cuts your carbohydrate levels so drastically to be sure you are healthy enough or not at risk for something else.

A serious risk worth discussing is called Ketoacidosis. It is lethal. It is caused by a deadly combination of metabolic acidosis, uncontrolled hyperglycemia, and increased ketones in the blood. This rarely happens to healthy people who are not diagnosed with diabetes. The majority of cases happen to those who have diabetes.

Ketoacidosis can develop very quickly, sometimes within 24 hours. Here is a list of common symptoms to watch for, so you know should you develop this dangerous disease.

- Resting heart rate above 100 beats per minute
- Dehydration
- Vomiting
- Drowsiness
- Blood glucose that is above 250 mg/dl
- Abdominal pain
- Blood pressure that is less than 90/60

If you experience any of these symptoms, especially if you have diabetes, then it more than likely you are experiencing ketoacidosis. You should go to the doctor right away and have yourself tested.

So what are some of the other risks worth mentioning? The keto diet may include increased risk of forming kidney stones, acidosis, which is high levels of acid in your blood, and for long-term use, it can cause drastic weight loss or muscle degeneration.

As discussed in the previous chapter, some of the immediate side effects that occur when you first start your diet may include constipation, low blood sugar, and sluggishness. Again, these occur during the first two weeks as your body adjusts to using ketones as energy instead of glucose.

Now, what about the mistakes we mentioned? There are three mistakes beginners often make while on the diet. The first is not getting enough salts which are sodium, potassium, and magnesium. While on a normal diet we typically get plenty of salt due to the amount of processed foods we consume. So when people switch to a keto diet and cut out those processed foods, they become low on sodium. When this happens, you may experience fatigue, and cravings, so be sure to watch your sodium levels. If you're an active person, replenishing your potassium is very important. You can add more potassium by eating potassium-rich foods like avocados and spinach. Magnesium is so important for sleep and mood as well as our muscles and general well-being, it is also good to make sure you are getting enough. Drinking bone broth is an excellent way to get some magnesium, as well as potassium and sodium.

The second mistake is not eating enough leafy greens. Many people think that low-carb means limiting their vegetables. However, it is actually needed to help in your digestion, especially with all the protein you will start consuming. Leafy greens also provide you with essential vitamins and minerals. There are many different ways to get more veggies into your diet including, sautés, salads, and smoothies. So eat your greens!

The third mistake people make on the keto diet is not exercising. Exercise is one of the most important components of a healthy lifestyle. It is also one of the easiest things to skip, especially when beginning a new diet, especially a low-carb diet like keto because you may be low on energy and mental stimulation as your body adjusts. However, if you can manage it, it's always good to do some form of exercise. Walking is one of the easiest options, but there are many other options out there like push-ups and sit ups.

The fourth and probably the most overlooked mistake people make is clean your kitchen out!
It so easy to fall into temptation, especially if their kitchens are still stock full of their favorite

temptation. Throw everything out including bread, pasta, cereal, popcorn, candy, and that secret bar of chocolate you always have hidden. Go to the grocery store and use your newfound keto genius and restock your fridge and pantry with proteins, veggies, and low-carb alternatives. It will make a difference in the long run.

Another good topic to discuss is how long should you stay on a keto diet? The answer is: however long you need to reach your weight loss goals. Some people switch back and forth between a Paleo diet for a few months and then back to a ketogenic diet as a way to stay healthy and continue for the long term.

Well, now that we have gone through everything you need to start your diet, let's get to the fun part! The next chapter contains the meal plan so you will be able to see what a month on a keto diet looks like.

Chapter 5
Ketogenic FAQs

Getting into a new diet plan can be challenging, not to mention, worrying. In this chapter, we will answer the most common questions people have about Ketogenic Diet plan.

Does keto diet plan have negative effects?
Unfortunately, yes. But for the most part, the negative effects you only have to deal with are tiredness, restlessness, and the hungry feeling especially in the first few days of the diet. This is normal. The reason is that the body doesn't have the fuel to get energy. The body is used to depend on carbs as a source of energy, and it goes completely crazy when carbs are taken away. This will not last for a long time. When the body realizes that it can use fat as an energy source, your energy will come back.

Here are other negative/side effects of keto diet plan:

- Headaches and dizziness

Headaches and dizziness may occur especially to those who are used to drinking coffee and other

sugar. Sugar and caffeine are both addictive, and if you stop taking them, you may feel dizzy and other withdrawal symptoms. The good news though is that the withdrawal symptoms will only last a few days and do not usually go severe.
So before you get into keto diet, you might want to slowly cut off your caffeine and sugar intake. This will help you avoid the withdrawal symptoms as much.

- Constipation

If you are not monitoring your micronutrients (vitamins, minerals, organic acids, etc.), you may experience constipation. This can make your diet plan difficult. But there's a simple solution to avoid constipation while on this diet.
Ensure that you consume most of your carbs from healthy greens that are rich in fiber. Also, drink a large amount of water. Water has been proven to fight and prevent constipation. If you are already experiencing constipation, try to take a laxative.

- Leg Cramps

Leg cramps usually happen at night and are more frequent to those who are in keto diet. And this is because, again, not watching the micronutrients. Leg cramps happen because there is not enough potassium in the diet plan. So, while in the keto diet, you want to make sure that you're eating foods with enough potassium. You can also try taking a supplement that has potassium, but that is not always suggested. It is still best to get potassium from real foods as they can provide you not just potassium but other nutrients the body needs.

- Bad breath

When in keto diet, you may experience bad breath. And no one wants bad breath, right? In keto diet, the body burns fat as a source of energy - and thanks to Ketones, an acid that helps break down the fat. However, the ketones released during the process can make the urine scent too strong and will give you bad breath.

The bad breath you will experience is not the same as you eat smelly food. To deal with this, try chewing gum without sugar, chew mint or parsley, or use mouthwash. These will help you get rid of bad breath while on keto diet.

None of these negative effects are life-threatening. True, they can be annoying and can make you feel uncomfortable, but there are ways to solve them.

Should I measure ketones?
It's optional. Some people measure the ketones they consume. Doing so is important to ensure that you achieve ketosis and stay in it to start losing weight. But again, it's not necessary, but it can be helpful. You can use testing strips to tell you if you have entered ketosis. You can bring these strips wherever you are to help you know if you are in the right range of carbs or not.

How will I know I'm in ketosis?
You can use testing strips to know your ketosis status. As an alternative, you can watch for symptoms. The body will show signs to tell you you're in ketosis. Some symptoms include increased thirst, bad breath, pungent urine scent, and loss of appetite.

Who can use Ketogenic Diet?
Most people who use ketogenic diet are those who want to lose weight. And that's basically because what keto diet does in the body. It uses fats as a

source of energy, and in no time, you can melt off the fat.
Ketogenic diet was originally designed to help patients with epilepsy or other neurological conditions. Studies found that keto diet help lessen the frequency of seizures. But now, the diet plan is also used by athletes.
We have discussed the health benefits of Keto diet in Chapter 2. Keto diet can fight off many illnesses, help one to slim down, and it makes one feel amazing. However, keto diet **is not for everyone.** These are the people who should avoid or not rely on ketogenic diet:

1. Expectant mothers and those that are breastfeeding
2. Those with thyroid glands problem
3. Children and teens
4. Athletes who need carbs to function better
5. Women with irregular menstrual cycles

Why? Because these group of people needs special dietary requirements. For example, an expectant mother needs carbs to help her baby grow. Eliminating the carbs, in this case, will result the baby to have nutrients deficiency. Another example, youngsters need glucose (which are found in carbs) in higher amounts than what the keto diet allows.

But that doesn't mean that these group of people cannot use some food plans in keto diet. For example, teens may choose to lower their carb intake a bit. They can also increase their intake of healthy fat and proteins.

If you are one of the groups above, you can talk to your physician and discuss if you can go with this diet plan. If not, they can give you better options for your health.

Can I do physical exercises while on Keto diet?
Yes. In normal circumstances, the body needs a high level of carbs to function properly and to be able to do physical workouts. And since ketogenic restrict carbs, you may be wondering if doing workouts is okay. Doing physical exercises is fine. But, in ketogenic diet, to truly lose weight, you need to focus more on what you eat, not in physical workouts. The foods you eat are what truly matters. You can start off with seafood, dairy, and meats. In this diet plan, you need to pay more attention to the quality of your diet. You need to know if your body is in ketosis. Knowing this will help you maintain your energy, thus helping you decide what physical workouts your body can do.

Why should I exercise while on Keto Diet?
Exercising (whether you're n keto diet or not) has several health benefits. It makes our bones stronger, it builds muscle, and it is good for the heart. Exercising while in the keto diet plan serves more benefits. Several studies have shown that keto diet (specifically, the process of ketosis) can help prevent fatigue for exercisers especially when they do long periods of aerobic exercises. What's more, it can:

1. Reduce blood pressure
2. Lose fat
3. Lose weight
4. Help you to be in better mood
5. Control blood sugar

What physical exercise can I do while on Keto diet?
There are four types of physical exercise that you can choose. Of course, what you will choose must

depend on your nutritional needs. These are the exercises you can choose:

- Anaerobic exercise

Anaerobic exercises are short-lasting intensive workouts. It demands oxygen that is more than what is available. Anaerobic exercises rely on energy sources, that means you need to take more carbs. Examples are weightlifting programs or HIIT.

- Aerobic exercise

Also known as cardio, this kind of exercise can be any activity that requires the heart to pump and stimulate heart rate. A low-intensity cardio workout is best for keto dieters. Some examples include swimming, kickboxing, dancing, running, and spinning.

- Stability

Exercises that help you balance and work more on your core are the kinds of activity Stability exercise endorses. These exercises are great in helping you control your movements, make your muscles stronger, and can improve your balance.

- Flexibility

Flexibility exercises can help stretch your muscles out, improve your mobility, and support joints. Stretching and yoga are examples of flexibility exercise.

Remember the *Targeted Ketogenic Diet* (TKD) we discussed in Chapter 1? You may want to consider that keto diet if you are planning to take intense physical workouts. TKD lets you eat carbs while on workout. But that doesn't mean you can go out and consume so much carbs from sodas and baked products. You have to get your carbs from keto-approved foods, and with TKD, you are allowed to increase your intake of carbs.

Can I take supplements while on Keto diet?
Absolutely, yes! But you should only take keto-friendly supplements. Taking in supplements is essential to supply enough micronutrients to the body while in keto diet, thus avoiding micronutrients deficiency.

What supplements can I take?
Here is a list of the supplements you can take:

Creatine: Creatine becomes a stored energy that your body can use very quickly. It is best for athletes and for those who lift weights. It also builds and strengthens muscles, as well as enhance performance. Not just that, studies have shown that creatine is also very helpful in aiding depression and neurological illnesses. It also has cognitive and anti-diabetic benefits. You can purchase this in food stores or on Amazon.

Fish Oil: You can purchase fish oil in pharmacies and health stores. It is available in liquid or in capsule. Fish oil has been found helpful in optimizing triglyceride levels (the source of energy when in ketosis). Triglycerides are essential to keep the body functioning while in ketosis, but too much of can increase the risk of cardiovascular diseases. Also, fish oil is rich in Omega-3 fatty acids - the best inflammatories there is.

Perfect Keto: This powdered drink supplement will provide extra ketones to your body. It can help you manage your ketosis, but it should not replace the keto diet. You should only take this when you exceed your carb limit. You can purchase this online at perfectketo.com

MCT Oil: Medium Chain Triglycerides, or MCTs, are fat molecules that are present in palm oil, yogurt, butter, and coconut oil. This fatty acid can be used as an energy source. Cool, right? When taking in coconut oil, for example, the body still have to work to separate the MCT from the other nutrients in the coconut oil. But with MCT oil supplement, the body has to work less and can get the MCT faster, thus supplying energy to the body quicker.

Chapter 6
30 Day Meal Plan

The following chapter contains a month's worth of meals for a ketogenic dieter and guidelines on how to plan it. It is important to note that this is just a guide, and not a rule, so feel free to personalize it however you like.

For example, some people may not like cooking 30 new meals, so they find a few they like and use them more frequently. Another good tip is cooking ahead. A lot of the omelets recipes can be used as muffin pan recipes, so you have taken along breakfasts or protein snacks. And chicken is a very versatile protein and baking or grilling several pieces ahead of time and refrigerating them allow you to have easy meal prep for lunch and dinner.

Everyone's needs are different, so if you need to increase your calories, increase your fats such as macadamia nuts, butter olive oil, and coconut oil are simple ways to get that calorie count up a little. If you feel you need to decrease your calories, you will need to decide what you need the most to stay in ketosis. Proteins are usually the easiest thing to lower, so watch your serving sizes.

Remember, you will want to try to keep your cheats to none. If there is a recipe in here you do not like, then, by all means, do not use it. And remember, it is always easiest to think ahead, planning to cook extra to be reusable throughout the week. As your body adjusts to losing its carb intake, keeping cooking to a minimum is a lot easier, and you do not have to think as much. Remember, a lot of the breakfast meals can be prepared grab and go style, so can be repeated throughout the whole first week, or even the whole month should you choose. Lunch can be prepared the same way.

The first month of keto dieting is the most important. This is what gets you into ketosis and begins your weight loss. Your diet needs to be the strictest during the first month. Once you have passed month one, your body will enter what's called nutritional ketosis, meaning your body has become keto-adapted. This means that your body is no longer in ketosis, but has become fully functional without its regular amounts of glucose. This is the ultimate goal of the ketogenic diet, and what will allow you to continue the diet easily. This process is different for everyone. It can take a few weeks, to a few months. Some of this depends on your genetic build, but also how strictly you adhere to the diet. Because of this, it is strongly recommended that you stick to the diet plan for 30 days, with zero to little cheating, because you want to reach the stage of keto-adaptation. Why? Because once your body has started using ketones proteins as the main source of energy, Adding excess carbohydrates will not affect it as much, and the process of getting back into a ketosis state does not take as long because your body is already used to using the ketones as its primary source of energy instead of glucose.

Before we look at the 30-day meal plan, here is a prime example of what your first four weeks will look like. Some of this may be a little repetitive after reading previous chapters. However, this will show you where exactly it all starts to fit into play.

WEEK 1 AND WHAT TO EXPECT

You've just cut all carbs down to a minimum. You can expect to notice the first signs of ketosis to show up as the keto flu, which we discussed earlier, in the form of fatigue, headaches, muscle aches, and moodiness. Please drink plenty of water and eat list of salt during this first transitional week. As your body adjusts, it will act as a natural diuretic, and you will be eliminating a lot of your electrolytes. Water and salt are key to helping those headaches as it replenished all those lost electrolytes. Make sure that you're drinking plenty of water, up to 4 liters a day, and eating plenty of salt.

Week 1 breakfast

Keep it simple. Make meals you can use multiple times. For breakfast make some of the muffin pan omelets included in the recipes at the end of the book, making it easy grab and go breakfasts. Hard-boiled eggs are a simple meal to prepare, packed with protein and fats, you can eat two or three for breakfast, or keep them with you as a snack.

Week 1 lunch

Keep it simple here too. Lunch will usually be a salad, so using leftover meat from previous night's dinner, or canned meat or tuna are very simple ways to make a sensible keto lunch. And do not forget lots of leafy greens and a nice high fat keto dressing should complete a rounded meal. It is also nice to prepare ahead, cook several pieces of chicken, or meat you like ahead of time and have in refrigerator to grab and be able to add to your lunches. If you choose canned meats, just remember to check for Additives and processed meats

Week 1 dinner

Dinner will be compiled of a hefty dose of protein like steak, a whole chicken breast or fish, with leafy greens Added as a side such as spinach, kale or broccoli. You can add fats to this by cooking the greens in it, and do not forget the salt to help replenish those electrolytes. Once again, planning ahead is fine, cook meals ahead of time if you need to so that if you are unable to prepare a fresh meal on a late work night, you have something easily accessible.

Remember, NO DESERT for the first two weeks of the keto diet, you need to get into that ketosis state, and you can't do that if sugars or excess carbs are introduced

WEEK 2 AND WHAT TO EXPECT

Ok, you made it through your first week and probably are in full blown keto flu. Remember, it will pass, and do not give up!

Week 2 breakfast

Keep breakfast simple again. If you found something you liked previous week, keep it up, it will help you survive the week and keep to the diet. We get to introduce something new this week. There is what is called heatproof coffee. This is a mixture of coconut oil, butter and heavy cream Added to your coffee. it sounds disgusting, but it can give you that Added fat boost you need as well as your caffeine most people drink. This idea is not so odd, butter is a big part of cream, so when you add it all to your coffee it's like drinking a nice decadent coffee. If this is something you think can do, awesome, if not then do not worry.

It's not for everyone.

But remember, any way you can add fats to this diet you are doing your body a favor, because you are now burning fat for energy, and eating fats help to increase your energy, and results in better weight loss. If you think you need to add some sweetener to the coffee to make it a bit more palatable, then stevia or Erythritol and vanilla extract may help you get it down a bit easier. Quick tip, if you are not used to eating coconut oil, take it easy because it is a natural laxative.

Week 2 lunch

Pretty much the same as week one. Keep it simple. Premade salads, lots of leafy greens, and lean proteins. Try lettuce wraps this week maybe, or your leftovers from the dinner the night before is an easy reheat in the microwave.

Week 2 dinner

Simple, simple, simple. Keep up the pace, and continue high-protein meals. The goal is to reach the end of the month, and you are half way there so do not quit now. And remember, if you need to add more to meal, add extra butter to your veggies, maybe an adventurous keto sauce this week to help liven things up. Again, no dessert this week.

WEEK 3 AND WHAT TO EXPECT

This week you should attempt an intermittent fast. It is not necessary but may be a good idea. It has been proven that fasting intermittently helps you stay in the ketosis fasting state. The goal here is to, if you choose to do this, is to eat a large, protein-packed breakfast, then do not eat anything until dinner time, attempting to keep 12 hours between meals. By doing this, we are now not Adding fats to our body, which forces the body to start using up the stored fats again, instead of the fats we are eating and Adding to the body. Again, this is only if you want to do this. It is not mandatory, and some people do this, and some do not.

If you find that you cannot go 12 hours without eating, then that is not a big deal, go back to week one basics and experiment with various other recipes as long as you lower your intake slightly.

Week 3 breakfast
Because the goal is to enter a fasting state, eating an excessively fatty breakfast will help sustain you through the day. Double the amount of keto coffee (if you are drinking it) or hey guess what? BACON! Bacon is an amazing source of fat and protein to add to your meal that will help you survive 12 hours of no food.

Week 3 lunch
If you are fasting, then no lunch, but your large fatty breakfast should still be keeping you going strong. A lot of people may hit the wall around 2pm, so drink plenty of water to keep you energized and feeling full. If you are not fasting, then a sensible lunch as in previous two weeks is fine, maybe a little on the smaller side to help your body use up some of the stored fat.

Week 3 dinner
Dinner is the same. A healthy part of it is protein and your vegetable. But surprise this week, even on the fast, you will get to add some bread to your menu. You can also start to have dessert in week three. If you choose. There are many die-hard ketogenic followers who are very strict and say absolutely no complex carbs or sugars for the first

30 days.

After all the research we have discussed throughout the entire book thus far, you should now be wise enough to decide which type of ketogenic diet you want to follow, whether you go full on die-hard nothing but the basics for 30 days, or a little less and decide to add some carbs this week, that is entirely up to you and your choice based on your weight loss goals.

WEEK 4 AND WHAT TO EXPECT

This week is slightly different again, or not, depending on the diet plan you choose. This week the fasting should get a little stricter again, and skipping breakfast and lunch is a good idea. Remember we are trying to get into full-blown ketosis, and then ketosis acclimated for month two. If you cannot fast, or are the type who cannot go without breakfast, then go ahead and follow week two goals again.

Do you see a pattern here? 1 week on, one week off? This keeps your body in a constant state of burning those fats for energy. It is highly recommended that you try to follow at least one of the fasts during the first four weeks. However nothing is set in stone, and everyone is different. A nice Added benefit to fasting is that it does help your self-control too. But, no big deal, either way, this is YOUR diet after all. Do what you need to help you stick to it!

This week you can add a little more desserts to the menu if you like, (again if you are following this plan, or not if you are going full throttle.)

Week 4 breakfast

If you are fasting, then no breakfast this week, drink

your coffee and lots of water. If not, return o week two diet plan.

Week 4 lunch
Lunch or no lunch, does not matter, but drink a lot of water. Remember, 4 liters a day is the recommendation while on a keto diet. If you are not fasting this week, again, return to week two lunches.

Week 4 dinner
If you are fasting, then dinner gets to be very large. Lots of proteins, fats, and vegetables. As well as nice healthy keto dessert. Add extra veggies if you wish to help keep you full.

WEEK 5 AND WHAT TO EXPECT
Congratulations! You survived your first month on a keto diet. This week is up to you, and where you start over again, either back to a semi-fasting state or slowly Adding more to your diet as you progress. Your diet, your rules, so while some return to week one if they have been doing plan one and no fasting over the month, keeping yourself in a steady state of ketosis, or you can repeat the two-week cycles of eating and fasting. You have made it to a keto acclimated body, and you should be feeling more mental clarity, energized, sleeping better, as well as hopefully met your first month's weight loss goals.

So, now that we have discussed week by week for the first month, here is what a 30-day meal guide looks like.

WEEK 1

Day 1 - Monday

B-Eggs With Scallions And Tomatoes
L-Pancetta With Brussels Sprouts
D-Garlic Cuban Pork

Day 2 - Tuesday

B-Sausage, Cheese, And Veggie Egg Bake
L-California Spicy Crab Stuffed Avocado
D-Grilled Steak With Tomatoes, Red Onion And Balsamic

Day 3 - Wednesday

B-Tomato Mozzarella Egg White Omelet
L-Philly Cheese Steak Stuffed Portobello Mushrooms
D-Chicken Thighs With Artichoke Hearts And Feta Cheese

Day 4 - Thursday

B-Muffin Omelet
L-Grilled Prosciutto Wrapped Asparagus
D-Grilled Salmon Kebabs

Day 5 - Friday

B-Veggie Ham Egg And Cheese Bake
L-Garlic Shrimp In Coconut Milk, Tomatoes, And Cilantro
D-Chicken With Mushrooms In A Garlic White Wine Sauce

Day 6 - Saturday

B-Eggs And Veggies
L-Zucchini Rolls
D-Crab Cauliflower Fried Rice

Day 7 - Sunday

B-Bacon And Eggs
L-Grilled Salmon With Avocado Bruschetta
D-BLT Lettuce Wraps

WEEK 2

Day 8 - Monday

B-Bacon And Eggs
L-Cobb Salads
D-Grilled Chicken Bruschetta

Day 9 - Tuesday

B-Tomato And Egg Omelet
L-Turkey Enchilada Stuffed Poblanos Rellenos
D-Braised Cubed Steak With Peppers And Olives

Day 10 - Wednesday

B-Avocado And Egg
L-Asparagus Egg And Bacon Salad With Dijon Vinaigrette
D-Grilled Chicken Salad With Strawberries And Spinach

Day 11 - Thursday

B-Baked Eggs With Wilted Baby Spinach
L-Pan Parmesan-crusted Chicken With Broccoli
D-Sheet Pan Shrimp With Broccolini And Tomatoes

Day 12 - Friday

B-Broccoli And Cheese Mini Egg Omelets
L-Burger Bites
D-Arugula Salad With Crispy Prosciutto, Parmesan, And Fried Eggs

Day 13 - Saturday

B-Guacamole Deviled Eggs
L-Buffalo Brussels Sprouts With Crumbled Blue Cheese
D-Pan Chicken With Bacon And Green Beans

Day 14 - Sunday

B-Loaded Baked Omelet Muffins
L-Grilled Steak Lettuce Tacos
D-Zucchini Carpaccio

WEEK 3

Day 15 - Monday

B-Fried Eggs
L-Burger Bites
D-Grilled Steak Lettuce Tacos

Day 16 - Tuesday

B-Hard Boiled Eggs
L-Sheet Pan Shrimp With Broccolini And Tomatoes
D-California Spicy Crab Stuffed Avocado

Day 17 - Wednesday

B-Hard-boiled Egg
L-Philly Cheese Steak Stuffed Portobello Mushrooms
D-Tuna Lettuce Wrap With Avocado Yogurt Dressing

Day 18 - Thursday

B-Sausage And Eggs
L-Pancetta With Brussels Sprouts
D-Grilled Garlic Chicken With Vegetables

Day 19 - Friday

B-Baked Omelet Muffins
L-Zesty Lime Shrimp And Avocado Salad
D-Grilled Flank Steak With Chimichurri

Day 20 - Saturday

B-Spinach, Feta, And Artichoke Breakfast Bake
L-Sausage Stuffed Zucchini Boats
D-Grilled Mediterranean Cedar Plank Salmon

Day 21 - Sunday

B-Asparagus Egg And Bacon
L-Cheeseburger Salad
D-Steak Kebabs With Chimichurri

WEEK 4

Day 22 - Monday

B-Open-faced Omelet With Avocado And Pico De Gallo
L-Enchilada Chicken Roll-ups
D-Braised Cubed Steak With Peppers And Olives Recipe

Day 23 - Tuesday

B-Arugula Salad With Prosciutto, Parmesan And Fried Eggs
L-Quick Garlic Lime Marinated Pork Chops
D- Grilled Chicken With Spinach And Melted Mozzarella

Day 24 - Wednesday

B-Baked Eggs With Wilted Baby Spinach
L-Mini Bell Pepper Loaded Turkey "Nachos"
D-Pancetta With Brussels Sprouts

Day 25 - Thursday

B-Guacamole Deviled Eggs
L-Buffalo Brussels Sprouts With Crumbled Blue Cheese
D-Baked Chicken With Dijon And Lime

Day 26 - Friday

B-Veggie Ham Egg And Cheese Bake

L-Cheeseburger Salad
D-Pan Chicken With Bacon And Green Beans

Day 27 - Saturday
B-Feta Artichoke Breakfast Bake
L-Chicken With Mushrooms In A Garlic White Wine Sauce
D-Grilled Flank Steak With Chimichurri

Day 28 - Sunday
B-Egg White Omelet
L-Mediterranean Chicken Kebab Salad
D-Chicken And Sautéed Collard Greens

WEEK 5

Day 29 - Monday
B-Loaded Baked Omelet Muffins
L-Grilled Tuna Over Arugula With Lemon Vinaigrette
D-Caramelized Onion, Red Pepper, And Zucchini Frittata

Day 30 - Tuesday
B-Sausage, Cheese, And Veggie Egg Bake
L-Cilantro Chicken Salad
D-Steak Sautéed Collard Greens With Bacon

Chapter 7
Recipes

The following are all the recipes included in the 30-day meal guide, plus more!

BREAKFAST RECIPES

Spinach, Feta, and Artichoke Breakfast Bake

It produces 8 servings and serving size is 0.25 slice. It contains:

- 11g Protein
- 7g Total Fat
- 128 Calories
- 1g Fiber
- Carbohydrates: 4g

What's in it

- crumbled feta cheese (0.5 cup)
- Chopped artichokes, drained and dried (0.72 of a cup)

- Diced red pepper (1/3 cup)
- Kosher salt (1.25tsp)
- Large eggs (8)
- Ground pepper (0.25 tsp)
- Grated Parmesan cheese (2T)
- Large egg whites (4)
- Chopped scallions (0.5 cup)
- Chopped fresh dill (1 tbsp.)
- Minced clove garlic (1)
- Far free milk (1/4 cup)
- Thaw and removed excess fluid from frozen chopped spinach (1, 10-ounce)

How it's made

1. Set oven to 375 degrees, prepare a baking dish with spray.
2. After mixing artichoke, garlic, red pepper, scallions, and spinach and dill, place all in a muffin pan.
3. Whisk the eggs, parmesan, egg whites, salt, milk, and pepper together. Mix them in feta cheese and add vegetables.
4. Bake 35 minutes.
5. Let cool 10 minutes

Loaded Baked Omelet Muffins

Produces 6 servings, with a serving size of 2 omelets. It contains:

- 165 calories
- 2.5g carbohydrate
- 20g protein
- 11g Total Fat

What's in it

- Nonstick cooking spray
- Kosher salt (0.25tablespoon)
- Black pepper
- Cooked chopped bacon (3 strips)
- Diced onions (3 tablespoons)
- Shredded cheddar (2 oz.)
- Thawed and drained frozen spinach (3 tablespoons)
- Large whole eggs (9)
- Diced tomatoes (3 tablespoons)
- Diced bell pepper (3 tablespoons)

How it's made

1. Heat oven to 375 degrees and grease muffin pan
2. Whisk eggs, season with salt and pepper.
3. Mix the remaining ingredients.
4. Fill up the tins and bake 20 to 25 minutes

Open-faced Omelet With Avocado And Pico De Gallo

This makes 1 serving and serving size = 1 omelet. It contains:

- 4g Carbohydrate
- 2g Fiber
- 140 Calories
- 9g Total Fat
- 11g Protein

What's in it

- Cooking spray
- Pico de gallo (2 tablespoons)
- Sliced avocado (1 tablespoon)
- large egg (1)
- Salt and pepper
- large egg white (1)

How it's made

1. Mix the egg and egg white and add salt & pepper.
2. On a medium to low heat, heat a medium nonstick pan. Spray it with oil and pour the eggs. Cook the mixture until they set, about 2 to 3 min then slide onto the plate.
3. Add the avocado and pico de gallo

Arugula Salad with Prosciutto, Parmesan and Fried Eggs

This recipes makes 2 Servings, Serving Size: 1 salad

- Calories: 344 calories
- Fat: 24g
- Carbohydrates: 8g
- Fiber: 1.5g
- Protein: 18.5g

What to use

- Five cups of baby arugula
- Fresh black pepper
- Olive oil spray
- 2 large eggs
- Four slices of sliced prosciutto (2 ounces)
- Shaved parmesan cheese (0.25 cup)

Dressing:

- Honey (0.25 tsp)
- Dijon mustard (2 tablespoons)
- Virgin olive oil (2 tbsps.)
- 2 tablespoon of minced shallots
- 1 tablespoon of sherry vinegar

What to do

1. Heat oven to 375 degrees. Place parchment paper on cookie sheet

2. Place prosciutto on the sheet and bake 15 minutes or until crisp.
3. Crumble into large pieces.
4. Whisk all dressing ingredients together
5. Toss arugula with dressing and divide on two plates and top with crumbled prosciutto and parmesan.
6. Cook the eggs in nonstick pan until whites are firm and yolk still slightly runny.
7. Place an egg on each salad and serve with fresh pepper, if desired.

Eggs with Scallions and Tomatoes

This makes 2 servings, and it can be prepared within 10 minutes.

- 2.3g Fiber
- 7.7 g Fat
- 155 Calories
- 8.5g Carbohydrate
- 13.9g Protein

What's in it

- 2 large Eggs
- I big diced tomatoes
- 4 diced scallions
- Salt and pepper
- Olive oil (1 tablespoon)

How it's made

1. In a heated pan, add olive oil, then cook scallions and tomatoes.
2. In a bowl, blend eggs, and season with salt and pepper.
3. Cook eggs in pan 2-3 minutes.

Broccoli and Cheese Mini Egg Omelets

It produces 4 servings, with a serving size of 2 omelets. Total time: 30 minutes

- 18g Protein
- 5g Carbs
- 8.5g Total Fat
- 167 Calories
- 1g Saturated Fat
- 2.5g Fiber
- 170g Cholesterol
- 0g Sugar
- Sodium: 317mg

What's in it

- Cooking spray
- Egg whites (1 cup)
- Broccoli florets (4 cups)
- Large Eggs (4)
- Olive oil (1 tablespoon)
- Cheddar (0.25 cup reduced fat shredded)
- Salt
- Fresh Pepper
- Cheese (0.25 cup good grated)

How it's made

1. Heat oven to 350 degrees.

2. Dice broccoli.
3. Cook the broccoli 6 to 7 minutes. Add oil, salt, and pepper.
4. Put broccoli mixture into a greased muffin pan.
5. Mix both types of eggs, salt and pepper, and cheese.
6. Pour eggs over broccoli.
7. Add the cheese and bake about 20 minutes.
8. Serve immediately.

Onion, Red Pepper and Zucchini Frittata

This makes 4 servings, and it can be prepared within 25 minutes.

- 243mg sodium (without salt)
- 1.6g Fiber
- 14.6g proteins
- 157.7 Calories
- 0.8g Sugar
- 9.3g Fat

What's in it

- Olive oil (2 tablespoons)
- Large eggs (4)
- Zucchini (one and a half cups diced into matchsticks)
- Salt and fresh pepper
- 4 Large egg whites
- Grated parmesan cheese (0.25 cup)
- White onion (1 thinly sliced rings)
- Diced red pepper (1 medium)

How it's made

1. Heat oven to 400 degrees.
2. Cook onion in pan with oil until brown
3. Add pepper and zucchini and cook 5 minutes more. Add salt and pepper and cook 3 more minutes

4. Whisk the eggs, egg whites, salt and pepper, and parmesan together.
5. Put eggs in the pan, covering all vegetables
6. Once edges darken, place pan in the oven. Cook 10 to 15 minutes more

Veggie Ham Egg and Cheese Bake

This makes 12 servings, with a size of 1 square. It contains:

- 14g Protein
- 102mg Cholesterol
- 1g Sugar
- 5g Carbs
- 8g Fat
- 1g Fiber
- 152 Calories
- Sodium: 385 mg

What's in it

- Red bell pepper (0.5 cup chopped)
- Olive oil spray
- Black pepper (0.25 tsp. ground)
- Egg whites(5 large)
- Milk (0.25 cup fat-free)
- Cheddar (2 cups shredded reduced-fat sharp)

- Kosher salt (0.5 tsp.)
- Broccoli florets (1 cup chopped)
- Ham steak (7 oz. finely diced lean)
- Eggs(7 large whole)
- Scallions (0.33 cup sliced)
- Mushrooms (5 oz. sliced shiitake)
- Tomatoes (0.75 cup diced)

How it's made

1. Heat oven to 375 degrees, grease a baking dish.
2. Put cheese in the baking dish.
3. Heat oil in a greased pan on medium, add red pepper, scallions, and mushrooms and sauté for 5 minutes more.
4. Add tomatoes, cook 2 minutes
5. Then add ham and broccoli and cook till done. Place over the cheese mixture.
6. Mix the eggs, salt, pepper, egg whites and milk, and whisk properly. Gently pour mixture over the vegetables in the baking dish and top with remaining cheese.
7. Bake 32 to 35 mins. Let it stand for 8 to 10 minutes.

Sautéed Collard Greens with Bacon

This recipes makes 4 servings

- Calories: 72.9
- Fat: 4.5 grams
- Protein: 3.1 grams
- Carb: 6.8 grams
- Fiber: 2.4 grams

What to use

- Olive oil (1 tbsp.)
- Bacon (1 slice chopped)
- Garlic (3 cloves chopped)
- Collard greens (1 bunch washed and dried)
- Salt

What to do

1. Remove stems, then slice into strips
2. Cook bacon on low in a sauté pan.
3. When bacon is cooked, add oil and garlic, sauté for a minute.
4. Add chopped greens to the pan, season with salt and place lid.
5. Simmer for 10 minutes, stirring occasionally.

SALADS AND ENTREES

Guacamole Deviled Eggs

This recipe takes 30 minutes to cook and prepare. It makes 12 servings, Serving Size: 1 egg

- Calories: 44 calories
- Fat: 3grams
- Carbohydrates: 2grams
- Fiber: 1gram
- Protein: 3grams

What to use

- Chile powder (for top)
- Eggs (6 large hard boiled)
- Cilantro (1 tbsp. fresh)
- Lime juice (3 tsp.)
- Red onion (1 tsp. minced)
- Jalapeno (1 tbsp. minced)
- kosher salt and fresh ground pepper
- Avocado (1 medium.)
- Tomato(1 diced)

What to do

1. Peel the cooled cooked eggs.
2. Slice into halves, set the yolks aside.
3. In a bowl, crush the avocado and egg yolks

4. Mix lime juice, jalapeño, cilantro, red onion, salt, and pepper. Add tomato.
5. Spoon guacamole into eggs.
6. Sprinkle with a little chili powder if desired.

Grilled Tuna Arugula Salad with Lemon Vinaigrette

This recipes makes 1 serving, Serving size: 5 oz. It can be prepared 8 mins.

- Calories: 297.8
- Fat: 15.5 grams
- Protein: 35.4 grams
- Carb: 3.8 grams
- Fiber: 1.6 grams

What to use

- Tuna (5 oz.)
- Extra virgin olive oil (1 tsp.)
- lemon juice(1 tsp. fresh)
- Arugula
- Capers(1 tsp)
- Kosher salt
- Fresh pepper

What to do

1. Season tuna with salt and pepper.
2. Arrange arugula and capers on a plate and drizzle with oil, lemon juice, salt, and pepper.
3. Set grill to high, and grease with spray.
4. Cook fish 1 minute.
5. Rotate and cook one more minute.
6. Cut tuna and place on top of salad. Top with lemon vinaigrette.

Chicken with Tomatoes and Rosemary

This recipe can be prepared in 7 minutes, one hour to cook and delivers 6 servings. It contains:

- 29.5g Protein
- 6g Carbs
- 7.5g Total Fat
- 1.5g Fiber

What's in it

- Fresh black pepper
- Chopped yellow onion (1)
- A pinch of Red pepper flakes (optional)
- Low sodium (2 cups)
- Chopped clove garlic (4)
- Chicken thighs (10)
- Chicken broth (fat-free)
- Kosher salt
- Butter (0.5 tablespoon)
- Chopped carrot (1)
- Dried Marjoram (0.25 teaspoon)
- Olive oil (.5 teaspoon)
- Crushed tomatoes (2 cups)
- Dry white wine (.25 cups)
- Fresh Rosemary (3-4 sprigs)
- Chopped stalk celery (1chopped)

How it's made;

1. Place a large pot on medium heat. Season chicken with salt and pepper. Add 0.5 tsp olive oil. When the olive oil is hot, place chicken and sear 6-7 minutes each side, until seared. Put this aside.
2. Add garlic, onions and red pepper flakes in remaining oil, keep on stirring occasionally until golden brown.
3. Add carrots, celery; cook on medium-low until soft.
4. Add chicken broth and wine.
5. Add marjoram, tomatoes, and reduce heat to low. Sprinkle salt and pepper and allow to simmer 30 minutes.
6. Add the rosemary and chicken to sauce, covering slightly to allow steam to escape, stir occasionally.
7. Cook on low heat for about 25 – 30 minutes.
8. Add water if needed.

Chicken Salad with Strawberries and Spinach

Makes: 4 Servings, Serving Size: 1 salad with 3 oz. chicken

- Calories: 331 calories
- Fat: 17g
- Carbohydrates: 4g
- Fiber: 4g
- Protein: 31g

What to use

For the dressing:

- Fresh black pepper
- of shallots (1 tablespoon)
- of water (1 teaspoon)
- Kosher salt (0.25 teaspoon)
- 3 tablespoon of extra virgin olive oil
- Honey (1 Teaspoon)
- 3 tablespoon of golden balsamic vinegar

To make chicken:

- Boneless and skinless chicken breast (16 oz.)
- 1 Crushed clove garlic
- 1 tablespoon of salt

To make salad:

- 3 cups of sliced strawberries
- Soft goat cheese (2 oz.)
- Six cups of baby spinach

What to do

1. Mix together all the dressing ingredients.
2. Season chicken with salt and garlic
3. Grill the chicken 10 to 11 minutes on each side.
4. Slice chicken on cutting board.
5. Toss spinach with dressing, chicken and strawberries and goat cheese.

Zucchini Carpaccio

This recipes makes 4 servings, Serving Size: 0.5 zucchini, 0.25 cup arugula, 2 tbsps. shaved parmesan

- Calories: 81 calories
- Fat: 6g
- Carbohydrates: 5g
- Fiber: 2g
- Protein: 3g

What to use

- fresh black pepper
- A cup of arugula
- 4 tsp of extra virgin olive oil
- 2 medium zucchini with ends removed and sliced 1/16 using mandolin
- Lemon (0.5)
- Shaved Parmesan (0.25 cup)
- Kosher salt

What to do

1. Combine oil and lemon juice. Create a zucchini layer to cover the bottom of a dish. Sprinkle with olive oil, lemon juice and salt and pepper.
2. Repeat layers until zucchini is gone.
3. Allow marinade to set for 10 minutes.
4. Serve topped with arugula and parmesan.

BLT Lettuce Wraps

Makes 1 Serving, Serving Size: 2 lettuce wraps

- Protein: 11grams
- Fiber: 2grams
- Carbohydrates: 8grams
- Fat: 10grams

What to use

- Four slices of center cut and diced bacon
- 1 tablespoon of light mayonnaise
- Fresh cracked pepper
- 1 diced medium tomato
- 3 large iceberg lettuce leaves

What to do

1. Pluck three large lettuce leaves from a head of lettuce.
2. Mix diced tomato with mayonnaise and pepper.
3. Put lettuce cups on a plate, fill with some shredded lettuce.
4. Add tomato and bacon and roll it like a wrap.
5. Serve.

Bacon Parmesan Spaghetti Squash

This recipe needs 7 minutes to prepare, 65 minutes to cook and will make 6 servings with a serving cup of 0.5. It contains:

- 6g Protein
- 7g Total Fat
- 1g Fiber
- 5.3g Carbohydrates
- 239mg Sodium

What's in it

- Medium spaghetti squash (1)
- Extra virgin olive oil (1.5 tablespoons)
- Bacon (4 sliced center cut)
- Kosher salt (1 pinch)
- Black pepper (fresh to taste)
- Parmesan (.5 cup course grated)

How it's made

1. Over medium heat, heat pan.
2. Cook bacon 5 to 6 minutes until crisp, then transfer to a paper-lined plate.
3. Oven is heated to 400F degrees.
4. Take a foil lines baking sheet and cut the squash in half end-to-end then scoop out the soft yellow strands and seeds with a spoon.
5. Sprinkle with salt and pepper to taste, then

put squash facing down onto baking sheet.

6. Bake for 60 to 65 minutes until the flesh can easily be pierced with a fork.
7. When squash is ready, add it with bacon, parmesan, and olive oil.

Pancetta with Brussels Sprouts

This recipe needs 8 minutes to prepare, 10 minutes to cook and makes about 7 cups, 9 servings with 0.75 Serving Size cup. It contains:

- 3.5g Protein
- 4g Fiber
- 9.5g Carbs
- 87 Calories
- 4g Total Fat

What's in it

- Grounded pepper
- Brussels sprout (2 lb.)
- kosher salt
- Extra virgin olive oil (1.5 tablespoon)
- Mined Pancetta, (2 oz.)
- Minced garlic (4 cloves)

How it's made

1. Shred Brussels sprouts with a sharp knife until finely shred.
2. Sauté pancetta on medium-low about 5 minutes in deep sauté pan, until pancetta becomes golden and the fat melts.
3. Add garlic and olive oil, sauté until golden. Then sauté on medium-high heat for about 5 to 7 shredded Brussels sprouts, salt, and pepper, until tender.

Cobb Salad

Makes: 2 servings, Serving Size: 1 salad

- Calories: 416 calories
- Fat: 23.6grams
- Carbs: 8grams
- Fiber: 3.4grams
- Protein: 41grams

What to use

- 2 cups of baby greens
- 2 sliced hard-boiled eggs
- Diced avocado (2 oz.)
- Cooked and crumbled bacon (4 slices; center cut)
- Quartered grape tomatoes (0.5 cup)

For the vinaigrette:

- Kosher salt (0.25 teaspoon)
- 1 tablespoon of Dijon mustard
- Chopped red onion (2 tablespoons)
- 4 teaspoons of olive oil
- Red wine vinegar (2 tablespoons plus 1 tsp.)
- Kosher salt (0.25 tsp.)

What to do

1. Mix Mustard, olive oil, red wine and salt in a

bowl and mix well, then add onions.

2. Chop the lobster into large chunks and place in different bowls
3. Add 1 cup greens in each bowl and top with eggs, bacon, avocado, tomatoes, and corn.
4. Drop 2 0.5 tbsp. vinaigrette over each salad.
5. Microwave the corn for 3 minutes if you like, grill 5 minutes or cook in boiling water for also 5 minutes.

Asparagus Egg and Bacon Salad with Dijon Vinaigrette

Makes: 1 serving, Serving Size: 1 salad

- Calories: 219 calories
- Fat: 13g
- Carbohydrates: 11g
- Protein: 16g

What to use

- Salt and pepper
- 1 teaspoon of red wine vinegar
- A bunch of chopped asparagus
- Cooked and crumbled center cut
- 1 large hard-boiled egg, peeled and sliced into two
- Dijon (0.5 teaspoon)
- 1 teaspoon of extra virgin olive oil

What to do

1. Boil a pot of water and cook asparagus until al dente.
2. In a small bowl mix the, oil, vinegar, Dijon and a pinch of salt and pepper.
3. Put asparagus on a plate, Sprinkle with dressing and bacon. Serve.

Tuna Lettuce Wrap With Avocado Yogurt Dressing

This recipes makes 2 servings, Serving Size: 2 wraps/ 2 tbsp. dressing

- Calories: 162 calories
- Fat: 5g
- Carbohydrates: 10g
- Fiber: 2.5g
- Protein: 20g

What to use

- Shredded or grated carrot (0.25 cup)
- Four large leaves of Lettuce
- Tomatoes (0.25 cup cherry quartered)
- 2 thinly sliced red onions, made into rings
- Four tuna that have been drained in olive oil
- 1 heart of palm, drained and sliced
- 2 tablespoon of avocado (with Yogurt Dressing)

For the Avocado Yogurt Dressing (makes about 2/3 cup):

- A tablespoon of water
- Lime juice
- A quarter teaspoon of kosher salt
- A clove of garlic

- Greek yogurt (0.5 cup 2%)
- Fine grounded pepper
- 3 tablespoons of freshly chopped Cilantro
- jalapeno pepper (0.5 seeds and membrane removed for mild heat)

What to do

For Dressing:

1. Blend all ingredients together in blender, adding more water to thin as needed.

To make wraps:

1. Place lettuce leaves on a plate and Top with hearts of palm tuna, red onion, tomatoes, and carrots.
2. Sprinkle each wrap with 1 tablespoon of dressing and eat right away.

Chicken and Cilantro Salad

This recipes makes 2 servings, Serving Size: 0.5 of

- Fiber: 0.2 grams
- Fat: 6 grams
- Protein: 23 grams
- Carb: 2 grams
- Calories: 163

What to use

- Chicken breast (7 oz. cooked)
- Mayo (2 tbsp.)
- Scallion (1 small chopped)
- Lime juice (2 tsp.)
- Cilantro(2 tbsp. chopped)
- Salt and pepper
- Garlic powder (A pinch)
- Cumin(A pinch)
- Chili powder(pinch)
- Chicken broth

What to do

1. Mix cilantro mayo, lime juice, scallions, and chicken.
2. Add salt, pepper, cumin, garlic and chili powders.
3. If chicken seems dry add 1 tablespoon chicken

broth as needed.

4. Put chicken in pot with broth, adding water if liquids do not cover chicken completely.
5. Add salt and pepper, whole stalk of celery; boil.
6. Lower and simmer 5 minutes.
7. Take from heat, tightly cover it, then let it rest 15-20 minutes.
8. Once cool, cut up chicken.

Zesty Shrimp and Avocado Salad

This recipes makes 4 servings, Serving Size: 1 cup

- Calories: 197 calories
- Fat: 8g
- Carbohydrates: 7g
- Fiber: 3g
- Protein: 25g

What to use

- A quarter cup of Chopped red onion
- 1 tablespoon of chopped cilantro
- Lime juice
- 1 teaspoon of olive oil
- 1 medium sliced tomato and avocado
- A quarter teaspoon of kosher salt
- 1 Jalapeno with seeds removed and sliced thinly
- Black pepper (0.25 tsp.)
- Jumbo cooked and chopped shrimp (1 lb.)

What to do

1. Mix olive oil, lime juice, red onion, salt, and pepper. Let it marinate 5 minutes.
2. Mix jalapeño, avocado, chopped shrimp, and tomato.
3. Mix ingredients together, add cilantro.

Zucchini Rolls

Makes 3 servings, Serving Size: 4 rolls

- Protein: 21grams
- Fiber: 5grams
- Fat: 17.5grams
- Carbohydrates: 18.5grams

What to use

- 1 large egg
- Garlic clove (1 minced)
- Skimmed ricotta cheese (0.66 cup)
- Chopped Basil (0.25 of a cup)
- Shredded mozzarella (0.75 cup)
- 1 tablespoon of kosher salt
- 1 cup of marinara
- Grated Romano cheese (0.5 cup, remain some for serving)
- 12 pieces of sliced zucchini (0.25-inch thick)
- Fresh black pepper

What to do

1. Set oven to 400 degrees.
2. Use a 13 x 9-inch baking dish to spread 0.25 cups marinara sauce on the bottom.
3. After this, cut the zucchini into 0.25-inch thick slices, to make about 12 slices.
4. Use salt and pepper to season both sides of

zucchini. Grill over high heat to dry out zucchini, until grill marks form, make sure it is not fully cooked for roughly 2 minutes each side.

5. Beat the egg and mix with basil, garlic, ricotta, Romano, salt and pepper.
6. Carefully spread ricotta mixture equally onto each zucchini slice.
7. Roll slices up and putt open side down in baking dish.
8. Place marina and cheese over each roll
9. Cover with foil.
10. Bake 20 minutes, cheese should be melted.

LUNCH RECIPES

Crab Cauliflower Fried Rice

Makes 4 servings, Serving Size 1.5 cups

- Protein: 29.5g
- Fiber: 5g
- Carbohydrates: 13g
- Fat: 8g

What to use

- 2 frozen king crab legs (approximately 1 lb.)
- Five diced scallions that have the green and white differentiated
- Riced cauliflower of 24 oz.
- 1 tablespoon of sesame oil
- 2 large eggs (beaten)
- Salt (a pinch)
- 1 diced small onion
- Cooking spray
- 2 minced garlic clove
- 3 tablespoon of soy sauce

What to do

1. To make cauliflower rice: cut into pieces, place 2 large heads of cauliflower into a food processor and pulse gently until a rice or

couscous texture appears

2. pour 2 inch of water into a pot, boil
3. Add the crab legs, and cook about 10 minutes covered.
4. After cooking, shell the crab and lightly flake it.
5. Heat a greased pan over medium heat, after, season eggs with salt. Add the eggs and cook, when ready, set aside.
6. First, reduce heat to medium-low, add the scallion whites, onions, sesame oil and garlic, sauté about 3- 4 minutes then raise heat to medium-high.
7. Add the soy sauce and cauliflower rice. Stirring occasionally, cook covered about 5 to 6 minutes. Cauliflower should be crispy
8. Add the crab and egg, top with green scallions, serve.

Garlic Cuban Pork

This recipe needs 8 hours to cook and prepare makes 10 servings, Serving Size 3 oz.

- Protein: 26.5g
- Fat: 9.5g
- Fiber: 0.5g
- Carbs: 2.5g
- Calories 213

What's in it

- Garlic (6 cloves)
- Bay leaf (1)
- Oregano fresh (0.5 tablespoon)
- Hot sauce
- Lime wedges
- Kosher salt (1 tablespoon)
- Lime juice (1 whole)
- Grapefruit (0.66 cup of juice from 1 grape, optional for serving)
- Cumin (.5 tablespoon)
- Salsa (optional)
- Pork (3 lb. boneless shoulder roast with fat removed)
- Tortillas
- Cilantro (chopped)

How it's made

1. Make sure to have a slow cooker.
2. Cut pork into 4 pieces and place into a bowl.
3. Put together grapefruit juice, oregano, garlic, cumin, lime juice, and salt and blend the combination until smooth.
4. Marinate the pork at least 1 hour or refrigerate overnight.
5. Put pork mixture into the slow cooker and then add a bay leaf
6. Cook on low for about 8 hours.
7. After Pork is cooked, shred pork with two forks.
8. Reserve liquid from slow cooker and set aside, then place the pork back into slow cooker. Add 1 cup of the liquid, season with salt to taste.
9. Keep warm until ready to serve.

Steak Kebabs with Chimichurri

This recipes makes 6 skewers, Serving Size: 1 skewer

Calories: 219 calories

Fat: 13g

What to use

- Bamboo skewers, presoaked
- Kosher salt
- 18 pieces of cherry tomatoes
- 1 red onion cut into big pieces
- fresh ground pepper
- Beef cut into 1-inch cubes(1 0.25 pounds)

For the chimichurri sauce

- 2 full tablespoons of chopped parsley
- 2 tablespoon of extra virgin olive oil
- Kosher salt (0.25 tsp)
- crushed red pepper flakes (0.25 teaspoon)
- 1 tablespoon of water
- I clove of minced garlic
- 2 full tablespoon of chopped cilantro
- Chopped red onion (2 tbsps.)
- Apple cider vinegar (2 tbsps.)
- fresh black pepper (0.25 tsp)

What to do

1. Season the meat with salt and pepper.
2. To make chimichurri, place all ingredients and Let marinade 5 minutes. Then add the rest of ingredients and mix. Refrigerate until ready to use.
3. Skewer the onions, beef, and tomatoes.
4. Grill on high to the desired doneness.
5. Transfer steaks to a serving dish and top with chimichurri sauce.

Grilled Salmon with Avocado Bruschetta

Makes 4 servings, Serving size: 1 filet

- Protein: 35.5g
- Fiber: 3g
- Carbohydrates: 7g
- Fat: 19g

What to use

- 1 tablespoon of extra virgin oil
- 2 medium-sized vine ripe tomatoes
- Freshly cut basil leaves (2 tbsp.)
- Black pepper
- Fresh cracked pepper
- Cooking spray
- 2 minced garlic cloves
- 1 tablespoon of extra virgin oil
- 1 small diced avocado
- 0.25 tablespoon of kosher salt
- Chopped red onion (0/25 cup)
- 1 tablespoon of Balsamic vinegar
- Four wild salmon filets (6 oz. each)
- Cooking spray
- Avocado bruschetta (to make 2.25 cups)

What to do

1. Mix salt, pepper onion, balsamic, olive oil, salt

let set 5 minutes.

2. Slice tomatoes and put with balsamic, garlic, basil, onion, salt and pepper, allow to sit 10 minutes.
3. Heat an already oiled gas grill to medium-high. (Oiling is only to prevent the fish from sticking oil the grates well)
4. Use salt and pepper to season salmon.
5. Place salmon with the skin facing down on the grill. Put the lid on, cook without turning for 8 to 10 minutes. If the skin blackens, this is ok because it will prevent fish from drying out.
6. Take salmon off the grill. Let it sit for 2 to 3 minutes.
7. Add the avocado to the bruschetta.
8. Top it with bruschetta and avocado and serve.

Turkey Enchilada Stuffed Poblanos

Makes: 4 servings, Serving Size: 1 poblano

- Calories: 233 calories
- Fat: 5g
- Carbohydrates: 13g
- Fiber: 3g
- Protein: 22g

What to use

For the poblanos:

- Cilantro sprigs
- Four large fresh poblano chilies
- Enchilada Sauce (1.5 cups)
- Diced scallions
- Colby-Jack shredded cheese (0.5 cup)

For top of the turkey:

- Canned tomato sauce (2 oz.)
- 93% lean ground turkey (12 oz.)
- Grounded cumin (0.75 tablespoon)
- Minced garlic cloves (2)
- Kosher salt
- Finely diced onion (0.25 cup)
- Grounded fresh pepper

- Medium chopped tomato (0.5)
- Cilantro (2 tablespoons)
- Oregano (0.25 tablespoon)
- Bay leaf (1)
- Chopped bell pepper (0.25 cup)

What to do

To roast the peppers:

1. Place poblano peppers on a flat surface to prevent rolling.
2. Cut peppers lengthwise, and scoop out seeds.
3. Roast peppers over grill until skin begins to blacken and blister.
4. Place poblano chilies into plastic bag to allow to steam for 10-15 minutes
5. Once peppers are cooled take a butter knife and scrape any blistered areas off of skin.
6. Heat oven to 350 degrees.
7. Pour 1-0.25 cups of the sauce into the bottom of a baking dish.

To make the turkey:

1. On medium heat, brown the ground turkey and place in large sauté pan. Season with the salt and pepper.
2. Add the cilantro pepper, garlic, chopped onions, and tomato, then continue to cook on low heat.

3. Add bay leaves, oregano, cumin, and more salt if desired.
4. Add 0.25 cup of water and tomato sauce and mix well. Lower heat cover and cook about 15 minutes.
5. Stuff about 0.5 cup of turkey mixture into every poblano pepper.
6. Place peppers face side up and top with sauce and cheese.
7. Cover and bake 30 minutes more until cheese melted.
8. Top with cilantro and scallions and serve.

Grilled Steak with Tomatoes, Red Onion and Balsamic

This recipe takes about 25 minutes to cook and makes 8 servings, Serving Size: 3 oz. steak, served with 0.5 cup salad

- Calories: 198 calories
- Protein: 25g
- Fiber: 0.5g
- Fat: 9g
- Carbohydrates: 3g

What to use

- Chopped red onion, (.75 cup)
- Fresh pepper
- Kosher salt
- Fresh oregano, basil or parsley (0.5 oz. each)
- Vinegar (6 oz. balsamic)
- 2 ounces of London broil steak
- Garlic powder
- 3-4 chopped Tomatoes (3.5 cups)
- Extra virgin olive oil (0.5 tablespoons)

What to do

1. Pierce steak all over with a fork and season with garlic powder, salt, and pepper then allow to sit at preferably room temperature for 10

minutes.

2. Add onions, oil, balsamic, pepper and salt in a large bowl. Allow onions salt and balsamic to sit a few minutes then add fresh herbs and tomatoes and adjust seasoning if you desire.
3. Heat the grill or boiler and cook steak on each side for roughly 7 minutes. This is done to good taste.
4. After time has elapsed, remove pork from grill or broiler and allow cooling for about 5 minutes before slicing.
5. Cut steak diagonally and make it thin, then top it with tomatoes and you are ready to serve.

Parmesan Chicken with Broccoli

Makes: 6 servings, Serving Size: 1 chicken breast with broccoli

- Calories: 334 calories
- Fat: 12.5g
- Carbohydrates: 4g
- Fiber: 2g
- Protein: 51g

What to use

- Minced garlic cloves (2)
- 2 tablespoon of olive oil
- Finely grated Parmesan cheese (0.5 cup)
- Boneless, skinless chicken breasts (6)
- 1 teaspoon of Kosher salt
- 12 ounces of fresh or frozen broccoli florets
- Chopped fresh parsley (0.25 of a cup)
- Garlic powder (0.25 teaspoon)

What to do

1. Heat oven to 425 degrees. Grease cooking sheet with 1 tbsps. olive oil.
2. Place chicken in baking sheet and arrange broccoli around it.
3. Sprinkle olive oil over broccoli and sprinkle all with pepper and salt.

4. Bake 25 to 30 minutes.
5. Mix together the Parmesan, garlic, and parsley.
6. Pour over each chicken. Broil 3 minutes, till broccoli is browning and cheese melts.
7. Remove from oven and let rest, then serve.

Grilled Garlic Chicken with Vegetables

This recipe needs 1 hour to season, 15 minutes to cook and makes 6 servings, Serving Size: 3 oz. chicken, 1 cup veggies

- Calories: 290 calories
- Protein: 28.5g
- Fiber: 3g
- Carbohydrates: 8g
- Fat: 16g

What to use

- Removed ends asparagus (1 lb.)
- Any herb marinade (1 pack)
- Medium-sized Zucchini (1)
- Boneless, skinned and thin chicken cutlets (1.5lbs.)
- Olive oil (cooking spray)
- Kosher salt
- Medium, sliced yellow squash
- Red bell pepper (1-seeded and sliced into strips)

What to do

1. Season chicken with 0.5 teaspoon of salt and 2 tablespoon of herb marinade of your choice and let it sit at least 1 hour, or overnight.

2. Marinate the veggies using the balance of your marinade.
3. Oil the grill and heat it over medium-high heat. Oiling is done to prevent sticking.
4. Place veggies on large grill tray (or 2 smaller trays) then season with 0.75 teaspoon salt and black pepper.
5. As you cook, to constantly keep turning for roughly 8 minutes until edges are brown, and then set aside.
6. Take about 4 to 5 minutes to grill chicken on each side until chicken is done.
7. Place on serving dish and serve with the veggies.

Sheet Pan Shrimp with Broccolini and Tomatoes

Makes: 4 servings, Serving Size: 7 shrimp

- Calories: 238 calories
- Fat: 11.5g
- Carbohydrates: 9g
- Fiber: 3g
- Protein: 26g

What to use

- Broccolini with the ends trimmed (12 ounces)
- 2 tablespoons of fresh lemon juice
- Kosher salt (0.75 tbsp.)
- A cup of grape tomatoes, halved
- 3 Minced garlic cloves
- Olive oil spray
- A pound of extra-large peeled and deveined, tail-off shrimp
- 1 teaspoon of chopped fresh oregano
- Fresh ground black pepper
- 4 tablespoon of extra-virgin olive oil, divided
- Minced garlic cloves (3)

What to do

1. Heat oven to 400 degrees.

2. Toss shrimp with 2 teaspoons garlic, 0.25 tsp salt, olive oil, red pepper flakes if using and black pepper.
3. Spray a large sheet pan. Spread broccolini and tomatoes evenly on the pan and Sprinkle with 0.5 tsp salt, 2 tbsps. olive oil, pepper, and oregano. Roast for 15 minutes, turning halfway through.
4. Remove veggies from oven then place shrimp around veggies.
5. Roast 8 minutes.
6. Pour lemon juice and serve.

California Spicy Crab Stuffed Avocado

This recipe needs 7 minutes to prepare, 15 minutes to cook and makes 4 servings

- Calories: 194 calories
- Protein: 12g
- Carbohydrates: 7g
- Fat: 13g
- Fiber: 4g

What to use

- Chopped fresh chives (one teaspoon)
- A lump of crab meat (0.25 oz.)
- Gluten-free soy sauce (two teaspoons)
- Light mayo (2 tsps.)
- Sriracha, for beautification (two teaspoons)
- Peeled and cut cucumber (1 cup)
- Hass avocado (1 small)

What to do

1. Mix mayo, sriracha, and chives in a bowl.
2. Tenderly toss crab meat, cucumber, and chives in a bowl.
3. Slice avocado and remove insides.
4. Use crab salad to fill the avocado halves equally.
5. To top up, add sriracha and extra soy sauce if you desire.

SNACKS RECIPES

Burger Bites

- Calories: 66 calories
- Fat: 2.5g
- Carbohydrates: 1.5g
- Fiber: 0.5g
- Protein: 8g

What to use

- Dill pickle chips or slice (30)
- 2 tablespoons of prepared mustard
- Kosher salt (0.5 teaspoon)
- 1 head of butter lettuce
- Minced center cut raw bacon (4 oz.)
- Onion powder (0.5 teaspoon)
- Ketchup, mayo and/or mustard (optional for serving)
- Cherry tomatoes (30)
- Beef (2 lbs. 93%)

What to do

1. Mix together with your hands the salt, beef, mustard, bacon, onion powder and pepper.
2. Form into 30 2 inch meatballs.
3. Grill on high for 3 minutes on each side.
4. Skewer with lettuce, pickles, and tomatoes and serve with ketchup and mustard for dipping.

Philly Cheesesteak with Portobello Mushrooms

Takes 7 minutes to prepare and 20 minutes to cook, makes 4 servings, Serving Size: 1 mushroom cap

- Calories: 256
- Fat: 16g
- Carbohydrates: 10g
- Fiber: 4g
- Protein: 19g

What to use

- Thinly sliced sirloin steaks (6 ounces)
- 4 medium-sized mushrooms (Portobello)
- Black pepper
- Light sour cream (0.25 cup)
- Diced onions (0.75 cup)
- Shredded cheese (3 oz. mild provolone)
- Soft, light, cream cheese (2 oz.)
- Light mayonnaise (2 tbsp.)
- Kosher salt (0.25 tablespoon)
- Green pepper (0.75 cup diced)
- Cooking spray

What to do

1. Set oven to 400 degrees.
2. Prepare a baking sheet with nonstick spray.

3. Remove mushroom stems and insides and then spray mushrooms with oil; season with 0.25 tsp. salt and fresh pepper.
4. Use salt and pepper to season the whole steak.
5. Allow the pan to get very hot, use a large pan, and spray with cooking spray place on high heat.
6. Add the steak, cook for not more than 2 minutes on each side.
7. After it is cooked through, slice it thin.
8. Reduce heat to medium-low, add more oil and sauté 5 to 6 minutes, until onions and peppers are soft.
9. Place all ingredients in a medium bowl, after this, transfer to mushroom caps, about 0.5 cup each.
10. Bake for 20 minutes, cheese should be melted and mushrooms tender.

Chicken Pesto Bake

Makes: 4 Servings, Serving Size: 1 piece chicken

- Calories: 205 calories
- Fat: 8.5g
- Carbohydrates: 2.5g
- Fiber: 0.5g
- Protein: 30g

What to use

- 2 boneless, skinless chicken breasts (or 16 oz.)
- Grated parmesan cheese (2 teaspoons)
- Pesto (4 teaspoons)
- Shredded mozzarella cheese (1.5 oz.)
- Fresh pepper
- Medium sliced tomatoes (1)
- Kosher salt

What to do

1. Slice chicken breast to make four slices. Add salt and pepper.
2. Heat oven to 400 degrees.
3. Put chicken on baking sheet. Spread 1 tsp pesto on chicken.
4. Cook for 15 mins.
5. Once done, garnish with both cheeses, and tomatoes. Bake 3 to 5 minutes more for cheese to melt.

Chicken Thighs with Artichoke Hearts and Feta Cheese

Takes about 40 minutes to cook, makes 6 servings, Serving Size: 1 medium thigh with artichokes

- Calories: 107.5 calories
- Protein: 16.5g
- Fiber: 1.5g
- Fat: 3g
- Carbohydrates: 4g

What to use

- 6 Skinless and boneless chicken thighs
- Fresh chopped parsley (2 tbsp.)
- Feta cheese (.25 cup)
- Salt
- 1 tablespoon of Oregano
- Optional lemon juice
- Fresh pepper
- 1 Crushed clove garlic
- 1 Marinated artichoke hearts (6 oz.)

What to do

1. Mix whole jar of artichoke hearts (liquid too) with chicken.
2. Marinade for 20 minutes. Then Drain all liquid.
3. Add salt and pepper, oregano, garlic.

4. Place pan 6 inches from the flame of boiler then boil on low heat until golden brown (takes 10 minutes).
5. Cook chicken 8-10 minutes on other side.
6. Use feta for the topping and boil one more minute.
7. After its ready, remove from oven and top with fresh parsley and lemon juice.

Grilled Prosciutto Wrapped Asparagus

Makes 4 servings, Serving Size: 4 spears

- Calories: 50 calories
- Protein: 4g
- Fiber: 1.5g
- Carbohydrates: 3.5g
- Fat: 2.5g

What to use

- 16 Asparagus spears with ends removed
- Olive oil
- 4 Slices of prosciutto
- Black pepper (to add taste)
- A pinch of kosher salt

What to do

1. Prosciutto should be sliced into 4 pieces and each piece wrapped around the center of each asparagus.
2. Cover lightly with olive oil, salt, and pepper.
3. Grill asparagus 5 to 6 minutes on low heat, covered, and turn every few minutes.

Mini Bell Pepper Loaded Turkey Nachos

This recipes makes 6 servings, Serving Size: 7 nachos

- Calories: 187 calories
- Fat: 11g
- Carbohydrates: 6.5g
- Fiber: 1g
- Protein: 18g

What to use

- Olive oil spray
- 1 teaspoon of kosher salt
- 1 cup of sharp shredded cheddar cheese
- 93% lean turkey
- Chicken broth (0.25 cup)
- Minced onion (0.25)
- Tomato sauce (0.25 cup)
- Light sour cream thinned with 1 tablespoon of water (2 tablespoons)
- Chopped cilantro, for top
- Mini rainbow pepper, cut and seeded (21)
- Thinly sliced jalapeno (1; optional)
- Sliced black olives (2 tablespoons)
- Minced garlic (1 clove)
- Cumin powder (1 tbsps.)
- Garlic powder (1 tbsps.)

- Chopped fresh cilantro or parsley (1 tbsps.)

What to use

1. Heat oven to 400 degrees.
2. Prepare baking tray with aluminum foil and grease.
3. Heat pan on medium and add oil.
4. Sauté onion and garlic and cilantro for 2 minutes.
5. Cook ground turkey, garlic powder, salt, cumin and cook 4 to 5 minutes until meat is cooked. Add tomato sauce and chicken broth, simmer on medium for about 5 minutes.
6. Arrange mini peppers cut side up in a single layer.
7. Fill with turkey mixture, and put jalapenos and cheese on top.
8. Bake about 10 minutes.
9. Top with black olives, sour cream, and cilantro.

Enchilada Chicken Rolls

Makes: 6 servings, Serving Size: 1 roll-up with 1 ounce avocado

- Calories: 261 calories
- Fat: 11.5g
- Carbohydrates: 8g
- Fiber: 3g
- Protein: 31g

What to use

- 1 tablespoon of cumin
- Mild green chilies (1, 4 ounces)
- Dried oregano (2 tablespoons)
- Chopped cilantro (for topping)
- 1 tablespoon of Garlic powder
- Mild red enchilada sauce (10 ounces)
- Far shredded Mexican cheese blend (1 cup)
- 1 large cubed avocado (6 ounces)
- Chili powder (0.5 tablespoon)
- Kosher salt (1 tbsps.)
- Fresh black pepper
- Cooking spray
- Skinless chicken breasts (1 ½ pounds (3) boneless, cut the length in half)

What to do

1. Heat oven to 375.
2. Mix the chili powder, cumin, garlic powder, oregano, salt and pepper in a bowl then rub mixture on each chicken piece.
3. In a small 8x6 dish grease with spray and then pour a small amount of enchilada sauce on the bottom.
4. Put the chicken on a work surface cut side up.
5. Put 2 teaspoons chilies and 1 0.5 tbsps. cheese on the chicken.
6. Roll up the chicken up and put open side down, cover with sauce, cheese, and chili.
7. Cover and cook 30 mins. Remove foil and cook 10-15 minutes more.
8. Serve each roll up with avocado topping.

Grilled Chicken Bruschetta

Makes: 4 servings, Serving Size: 2 cutlets

- Calories: 237 calories
- Fat: 8.5g
- Carbohydrates: 7g
- Fiber: 1g
- Protein: 32g

What to use

- Medium vine ripe tomatoes (3)
- Balsamic vinegar (1 tablespoon)
- Thinly sliced chicken cutlets (1.25 lbs. or 8 pieces)
- Small minced cloves garlic cloves (2)
- Kosher salt
- Chopped red onion (0.25 cup)
- Fresh cracked pepper to taste
- Chopped fresh basil leaves (2 tablespoons)
- I tablespoon of extra virgin oil
- Diced skim mozzarella (3 oz.)

What to do

1. Mix onion, olive oil, balsamic, 0.25 tsp. together in a bowl, add kosher salt and pepper. Put this aside for a few minutes.

2. Cut tomatoes and place in a large bowl with onion-balsamic mix, garlic, basil and add salt and pepper to your liking. Let it sit 10 minutes.
3. Use salt and fresh pepper to season chicken.
4. Heat the grill, set the temperature to medium-high.
5. Place chicken on the grill for 2 minutes. When ready, set aside on serving dish and top with bruschetta.

Cheeseburger Salad

This recipes makes 4 Servings, Serving Size: 1 salad

- Calories: 314 calories
- Fat: 19g
- Carbohydrates: 10g
- Fiber: 4g
- Protein: 28g

What to use

For the salad

- Chopped dill pickle spears (4)
- Grounded black pepper
- Reduced-fat shredded cheddar cheese (0.25 cup)
- Cubed avocado (obtained from one small has)
- 1 pound of 93% lean ground beef
- (0.25 tsp) kosher salt
- Red onion sliced into rings (0.5)
- A cup of cherry tomatoes
- 4 cups of chopped romaine lettuce

For the dressing

- Garlic powder (0.25 tablespoon)
- Paprika (0.25 tsp)
- Onion powder (0.25 teaspoon)

- Four teaspoons of ketchup
- 1 teaspoon of mustard
- Light mayonnaise (0.25 cup)
- A teaspoon of dill pickle juice

What to do

1. Combine beef, salt, and pepper in a bowl then make four patties
2. Whisk together dressing ingredients. Set aside.
3. Grill hamburger around 4-5 minutes per side. Add onion rings. Cook onion 4 to 5 minutes, turning at halfway point.
4. Let patties cool, then slice into 16 pieces.
5. Add avocado, lettuce, onion, pickles, and tomato.
6. Place everything on a plate and top with grilled onions, cheese, and hamburger. Sprinkle with 0.25 of the dressing.

Chicken with Bacon and Green Beans

This recipes makes 4 Servings, Serving Size: 3 oz. chicken, 0.5 cup green beans

- Calories: 211 calories
- Fat: 5g
- Carbohydrates: 7g
- Fiber: 2g
- Protein: 29g

What to use

- Eight ounces of French green beans
- 2 tablespoon of minced shallot
- 1 teaspoon of chopped fresh thyme
- Kosher salt
- Grounded black pepper
- 2 minced garlic cloves
- Low-sodium broth (0.75 cup)
- A pound of boneless, skinless chicken breasts, cut into thin pieces
- Crisp white wine (0.5 cup)
- Center-cut bacon chopped into 4 strips

What to do

1. Over medium-high heat cook bacon. Take away bacon pieces and set aside.
2. Season chicken with salt and black pepper,

add to the pan and cook 4 minutes each side, or until cooked through.

3. In now empty pan place shallots and sauté 1 minute. Make sure to scrape any bits on bottom up.
4. Add the garlic heat until brown.
5. Pour in the thyme, broth, and wine.
6. Increase heat, add the green beans, and cook for about 8 minutes, giving an occasional stir.
7. Transfer the chicken breasts and green beans to a serving dish. Add salt and pepper to taste.
8. Serve chicken topped with sauce and green beans.

Grilled Steak Lettuce Tacos

This recipes makes 4 servings, Serving Size: 2 tacos

- Calories: 256 calories
- Fat: 14g
- Carbohydrates: 7g
- Fiber: 3g
- Protein: 25g

What to use

For Pico de Gallo

- Cup diced tomato (0.5)
- Kosher salt (0.25 tablespoon)
- Chopped onion (0.25 cup)
- 1 tablespoon of lime juice
- I tablespoon of minced jalapeno
- 1 tablespoon lime juice

For the guacamole

- I small avocado
- Kosher salt (0.5 tsp)
- Fresh black pepper, to taste
- 2 teaspoons of lime juice
- Diced tomato (0.25 cup)
- 2 tablespoons of diced red onion

- Chopped cilantro (2 teaspoons)

For the steak

- Dried oregano (0.25tsp)
- Eight lettuce shells
- A teaspoon of kosher salt
- A pinch of fresh grounded pepper
- Thin sirloin steaks (1 lb.)
- 1 teaspoon of ground cumin(1 tsp)
- Garlic powder (0.5 tsp)

What to do

1. Rub the salt, cumin, garlic powder, oregano and black pepper over the steak.
2. Mix all guacamole ingredients in a bowl and mash well.
3. Mix the pico de gallo ingredients.
4. Heat a grill to high. Cook the steaks on each side 2 to 3 minutes, or until the steak is cooked to your liking.
5. Slice into thin strips.
6. To serve, fill each lettuce cups with 0.5 tbsps. guacamole and top with steak and pico de gallo.

Sausage Stuffed Zucchini with Mozzarella Cheese

This recipes makes 8 servings, Serving Size: 1 boat

- Calories: 153 calories
- Fat: 7g
- Carbohydrates: 9g
- Fiber: 2g
- Protein: 13g

What to use

- 1 cup of Marinara sauce
- Finely cut small onions (0.5 cup)
- 8 tsps. grated Parmesan cheese
- Diced Red bell pepper (0.5 cup)
- Italian chicken sausage (14 oz. lean removed from casing)
- A teaspoon of oil
- Four medium zucchini (31 oz. in total)
- Finely cut onion (0.5)
- 3 cloves crushed garlic
- 8 teaspoons grated Parmesan cheese

What to do

1. Boil a large pot of water
2. Heat oven to 400 degrees.

3. Cut zucchini in half, and remove insides, chop the insides of the zucchini and set aside.
4. Boil zucchini for 1 minute.
5. Place 0.25 cup of sauce in the dish, and set zucchini open side up
6. In a large pan, cook sausage.
7. Cook oil and add onion, garlic and bell pepper for 2-3 minutes.
8. Add zucchini insides, season with salt and pepper and cook 2-3 minutes.
9. Add sausage and cook 3 more minutes.
10. Fill each empty zucchini cooked sausage, pressing firmly.
11. Top each with sauce mozzarella cheese and parmesan cheese.
12. Bake in a foil covered dish 35 minutes

DINNER RECIPES

Grilled Salmon Kebabs

Makes: 4 servings, Serving Size: 2 kebabs

- Calories: 267 calories
- Protein: 35g
- Fiber: 3g
- Carbohydrates: 7g
- Fat: 11g

What to use

- 2 tablespoons of fresh chopped oregano
- Olive oil cooking spray
- 2 tablespoons of sesame seeds
- 1 tablespoon of grounded cumin
- 0.25 teaspoon of crushed red pepper flakes
- Skinless wild salmon fillet (weighing 1.5 lbs. diced into 1-inch pieces)
- 2 thinly sliced lemon rounds
- 1 tablespoon of kosher salt
- Sixteen bamboo skewers (to be soaked in water for at least 1 hour)

What to do

1. Heat grill on medium heat and then do not forget to spray with nonstick spray.
2. Mix sesame seeds, oregano, red pepper and cumin.

3. Starting with a salmon piece, and being sure to end with a salmon piece, thread salmon and folded lemon slices onto 2 kebab sticks each, creating total of 8 kebabs.
4. Use the spice mixture to season fish kebabs and lightly spritz with oil
5. Place kebabs on grill, turning it occasionally until fish is opaque, 10 minutes.

Brussels Sprouts with Crumbled Blue Cheese

This recipes makes 4 Servings, Serving Size: 0.75 cup

- Calories: 123 calories
- Fat: 8g
- Carbohydrates: 10g
- Fiber: 4g
- Protein: 5g

What to use

- (0.25) cup Franks Hot Sauce
- 2 tablespoons of crumbled blue cheese. Used for topping.
- 2 tablespoon of olive oil
- Brussels sprouts, trimmed and halved

What to do

1. Heat oven to 425 degrees. Heat an oven-safe pan on medium-high.
2. Add olive oil and Brussels sprouts. let cook without turning for 3 minutes until browned. Turn occasionally for an Additional 2-3 minutes until brown all over.
3. Move the whole pan to oven and roast for 8-10 minutes, until softened a bit but still firm.
4. Top with blue cheese and hot sauce.

Garlic and Lime Pork Chops

This recipes makes 4 Servings, Serving Size: 1 chop

- Calories: 224 calories
- Fat: 6g
- Carbohydrates: 1.8g
- Fiber: 0g
- Protein: 38g

What to use

- 1 teaspoon of kosher salt
- 1 teaspoon of lime zest
- Cumin (0.5 tsp)
- Lime juice (0.5)
- 4 lean boneless pork chops (6 oz. Each)
- 1 teaspoon of fresh pepper
- Chili powder (0.5 tsp)
- 4 cloves of crushed garlic
- Half teaspoon of paprika
- 1 teaspoon of fresh pepper

What to do

1. Remove fat from pork, then season pork with chili powder, paprika, garlic, cumin, salt, and pepper. Add lime zest and the juice; marinate at least 20 minutes.
2. To broil: broil pork 4-5 minutes on each side.

Grilled Mediterranean Cedar Plank Salmon

This recipes makes 4 servings, Serving Size: 0.25 of the salmon

- Calories: 251 calories
- Fat: 11g
- Carbohydrates: 8g
- Fiber: 2g
- Protein: 30g

What to use

- 1 cup of tomato
- Black pepper
- Fresh oregano and thyme (optional for top)
- A quarter kosher salt
- A quarter sliced red onion
- 1 untreated cedar plank
- 1 teaspoon of red wine vinegar
- 1 teaspoon of olive oil
- 1 teaspoon of dried onion
- 0.25 cup of Kalamata
- 1 Boneless wild salmon fillet
- 1/2 lemon
- A teaspoon of dried oregano
- Tomatoes (1 cup grape halved)

What to do

1. Slice half the lemon. Season fish with oregano, salt, other half of lemon, and black pepper.
2. Combine the red onion, olive oil, tomatoes, vinegar, olives, salt, and pepper.
3. On the presoaked plank, put salmon and herbs, skin side down. Put lemon slices on top.
4. Heat the grill to medium-high.
5. Place planked salmon on direct heat for 3 to 4 minutes, until the planks start to smoke.
6. Move plank to other side of grill where no direct heat is in contact, and grill 12 to 15 minutes.
7. Top with tomato mix and serve.

Braised Cubed Steak with Peppers and Olives Recipe

Makes: 8 servings, Serving Size: per steak with sauce

- Calories: 154 calories
- Protein: 23.5g
- Fiber: 1g
- Fat: 5.5g
- Carbohydrates: 4g

What to use

- Green pitted olive leaves (0.033 of a cup and 2 tablespoons of brine)
- 1 sliced small red pepper
- Black pepper
- Cubed steak (28 oz.)
- A cup of water
- 1 tsp. of adobo seasoning or garlic salt
- 1 canned tomato sauce (8 oz.)
- Sliced, medium-sized onion (half)

What to do

1. Season beef with adobo, garlic salt, and black pepper to taste
2. Place into slow cooker.
3. Pour all ingredients over pork.
4. Cook 8 hours on low.

Chicken with Mushrooms with Garlic White Wine Sauce

Makes 8 tenderloins, Serving Size: 2 tenderloins with mushrooms

- Calories: 217 calories
- Protein: 29.5g
- Fat: 7.5g
- Carbohydrates: 6g
- Fiber: 1.5g

What to use

- Eight or 16 oz. chicken tenderloins
- 2 teaspoons of Olive oil
- Minced garlic cloves (3)
- White wine (0.25 cup)
- Fresh parsley (0.25 cup)
- Flour (0.25 cup)
- Mushrooms (12 oz. sliced)
- chicken broth, fat-free (.33 cup)
- Salt and pepper
- 2 teaspoons of butter

What to do

1. Make sure to heat oven to 200 degrees.
2. Using the salt and pepper, season chicken and gently coat in flour.

3. Add 1 tsp. butter and 1 tsp. olive oil preheated pan.
4. Add chicken and on medium heat cook for about 5 minutes then place in oven to keep warm.
5. Add rest of oil and butter, add garlic and let it heat until garlic opaque, Add mushrooms with salt and pepper cook until golden, stirring occasionally.
6. Add chicken broth, wine, and parsley, and stir the pan to mix up any brown pieces from the bottom of the pan.
7. Boil until fluid reduces by half.
8. Serve chicken topped with mushroom sauce.

Coconut Milk Shrimp with Tomatoes and Cilantro

Makes 4 servings, Serving Size 1.5 cups

- Calories: 267 calories
- Protein: 30g
- Fat: 10.5g
- Carbohydrates: 9.5g
- Fiber: 1.5g

What to use

- 4 thinly cut scallions that have the white and green parts differentiated
- 1 tablespoon of olive oil
- 4 Minced garlic cloves
- 1 diced red bell pepper
- Squeezed lime (0.5)
- Chopped cilantro (0.5 cup)
- Crushed red pepper flakes (0.5 tablespoon)
- Light coconut milk (14 oz.)
- Diced tomatoes (14.5 oz.)
- 0.5 tablespoon of Kosher salt
- Peeled jumbo shrimp (1.25 lbs. after peeling)

What to do

1. Heat oil on medium-low heat in a medium pot.
2. Add red peppers and cook to softness.

3. Add garlic and red pepper flakes, scallion whites, .25 cup cilantro, and heat 1 minute.
4. Add jar of tomatoes, coconut milk, and 0.25 tsp. salt. Allow heat to increase until boiling.
5. Reduce heat to low, cover and let simmer for about 10 minutes to make the sauce thick.
6. Add shrimp and cook until shrimp is opaque (clear).
7. Add lime juice.
8. You can then divide equally among 4 bowls, each bowl having 1.25 cups then top with cilantro and remaining scallions to give it a nice look.

Grilled Flank Steak with Chimichurri

This recipes makes 6 servings, Serving Size: 3 ounces steak with 4 tsp sauce

- Calories: 232 calories
- Fat: 14g
- Carbohydrates: 1g
- Fiber: 0g
- Protein: 24g

What to use

- 1 steak (0.5 pounds flank)
- Dried oregano (0.5 teaspoon)
- 1 kosher salt (0.25 tablespoon)
- Fresh ground pepper
- 1 tablespoon of garlic powder
- Grounded cumin (0.75 teaspoon)

For the Chimichurri Sauce:

- 1 tablespoon of water
- 2 tablespoon parsley, finely cut
- Fresh black pepper (0.25 tsp.)
- Apple cider vinegar (2 tbsps.)
- Red onion (2 tbsps. chopped)
- Cilantro (2 tbsps.)
- Kosher salt (0.25 teaspoon)

- Red pepper flakes (0.25 tsp crushed)
- 1 minced Garlic clove
- Extra virgin olive oil (2 tbsps.)

What to do

1. Lightly score the steak on both sides.
2. Mix the garlic powder, ground pepper, cumin, oregano, and kosher salt. Season both sides of the steak.
3. Mix the vinegar, salt olive oil, and red onion, and let marinate about 5 minutes. Add all other ingredients and mix.
4. Set grill to high. Grill the steaks to desired doneness.
5. Let steaks cool 5 minutes. Slice steaks into thin strips.
6. Set on serving dish and top with chimichurri sauce.

Chicken with Dijon and Lime

This recipes makes: 4 servings, Serving Size: 2 drumsticks

- Calories: 172 calories
- Fat: 5g
- Carbohydrates: 4g
- Fiber: 0g
- Protein: 26g

What to use

- chicken drumsticks (8 skin removed)
- Dijon mustard (3 tbsp.)
- Mayo (1 tbsp.)
- Garlic (1 clove crushed)
- Lime zest (1 squeezed)
- Black pepper (0.75 tsp.)
- kosher salt to taste
- parsley (1 teaspoon dried)

What to do

1. Heat oven to 400 degrees
2. Set chicken, skin and fat removed, in a large bowl and season with salt.
3. Mix all ingredients except parsley. Mix well. Pour over chicken, coat well.
4. Prepare baking dish with spray.
5. Arrange chicken in one layer and garnish with

parsley.

6. Bake 35 minutes. Put chicken under broiler about 3 minutes to crisp.

Grilled Chicken with Spinach and Melted Mozzarella

This recipes makes 6 Servings, Serving Size: 1 piece

- Calories: 195 calories
- Fat: 6g
- Carbohydrates: 3.5g
- Fiber: 1.5g
- Protein: 31g

What to use

- Chicken breasts(24 oz. (3 large) sliced in half lengthwise to make 6)
- Kosher salt and pepper
- Olive oil (1 tsp.)
- Garlic (3 cloves crushed)
- Spinach (10 oz. frozen drained)
- Mozzarella(3 oz. shredded)
- Red pepper (0.5 cup roasted sliced in strips (packed in water)
- Olive oil spray

What to do

1. Heat oven to 400 degrees. Season chicken with salt and pepper. Cook chicken in a prepared nonstick pan, until no longer pink, about 2 to 3 minutes per side.
2. On medium heat cook oil, and garlic for 30 seconds. Add spinach, salt, and pepper. Cook 2 to 3 minutes.
3. Place chicken on a cookie sheet, separate spinach between chicken and place on top.
4. Top each with 0.5 oz. mozzarella, roasted peppers and bake until melted, about 3 minutes.

DESSERTS

Flourless Keto Brownies

This recipes makes 16 Flourless Keto Brownies

- Calories: 87 calories
- Fat: 8g
- Carbohydrates: 2.9g
- Proteins: 2g
- Fiber: 2.4g

What to use

- Milk chocolate (Low-carb 5 ounces)
- Mascarpone cheese (.25 cup)
- Cocoa powder (.25 cup unsweetened)
- Salt (.5 tsp.)
- Butter (4 tablespoons)
- Eggs (3 large)
- Low-carb sweetener of your choice (truvia, stevia, etc.) (.5 cup)

What to do

1. Preheat oven to 375 degrees. Melt 5 oz. chocolate over hot water in a glass bowl for 30 times, stirring each time until no longer chunky.
2. Add butter to chocolate and microwave for 10 seconds. Stir. Repeat until smooth. Allow to cool.

3. In a large bowl, beat three eggs and ½ cup granulated sweetener on high until the mixture becomes frothy and the eggs become pale. This should take about 3-5 minutes.
4. Add the mascarpone cheese and beat until smooth.
5. Sift in half of the cocoa powder and ½ tsp salt and gently mix. The power will resist mixing with the egg so go slow and keep at it.
6. Sift in the rest of the cocoa powder and stir until all of the mixture is dissolved and the batter forms.
7. Make sure your chocolate is still melted. If not, heat for 10 seconds and stir.
8. Fold the melted chocolate into the batter and mix well until it is creamy and there are no lumps.
9. Pour batter into prepared 8×8 pan and bake 25 mins
10. Remove from pan and let cool before cutting

Coconut Chocolate Chip Cookies

This recipes makes 16 Low-carb Coconut Chip Cookies

- Calories: 431 calories
- Fats: 17.5g
- Carbohydrates: 2.25g
- Protein: 4.7g
- Fiber: 2g

What to use

- Liquid stevia (25 drops)
- Almond flour (1 cup)
- Butter, melted (.25 cup)
- Cocoa nibs (1 cup)
- Stevia (.33 cup)
- Salt (.25 tsp.)
- Coconut flakes (.5 cup V)
- Almond butter (.5 cup)
- Large eggs (2)
- Glaze (optional):
- Liquid stevia (10 drops)
- Heavy whipping cream (.25 cup)
- Vanilla extracts (.5 tsp.)

What to do

1. Heat oven to 350. Mix together all dry

ingredients, cacao nibs, almond flour, coconut flakes Erythritol and salt.

2. Mix together all of the wet ingredients, almond butter, melted butter, eggs and liquid stevia.
3. Slowly add dry ingredients to wet ingredients until they are mixed completely.
4. Spoon batter onto a prepared sheet.
5. Squash the cookie dough with a spoon, till about 0.25 inch thick.
6. Bake cookies for 20- 25 mins, until golden brown.
7. Allow to cool before glazing.
8. For Glaze: mix the heavy cream, sweetener, and extract using a small hand blender.
9. Put glaze into refrigerator to thicken, then glaze over cookies.

Keto Pound Cake

This recipes makes 16 servings

- Calories: 254.2 calories
- Protein: 8g
- Carbohydrates: 2.5g
- Fats: 23g
- Fiber: 1.9g

What to use

Pound cake

- Cream cheese (8 oz.)
- Baking powder (1.5 tsp.)
- Salt (.5 tsp.)
- Vanilla extract (1.5 tsp)
- Lemon extract (.5 tsp.)
- Almond flour (2.5 cups)
- Erythritol (a non-sugar sweetener 1.5 cups)
- Butter (unsalted softened .5 cup)
- Eggs (whole room temperature (8)
- Glaze
- Vanilla extracts (.5 tsp.)
- Cream (3 tsp. heavy whipping)
- Powdered erythritol (.25 cup)

What to do

1. Heat oven to 350 degrees.
2. Combine together cream cheese, butter, and erythritol.
3. Blend together butter and erythritol until smooth. Next, add chunks of softened cream cheese; blend together till no longer chunky.
4. Add the eggs, lemon and vanilla extracts to the blended ingredients. Continue blending with a hand mixer until smooth.
5. Mix almond flour, salt, and baking powder.
6. Slowly add dry ingredients to the batter. Continue blending until batter is smooth. Then empty batter into loaf pan.
7. Bake 60 minutes or longer, when a tester comes out clean.

If creating glaze:

1. Mix together the vanilla extract, powdered erythritol, and heavy whipping cream until smooth. Wait until pound cake is completely cool before spreading the glaze on top.

Cinnamon Pecan Bars

This recipes makes 16 bars, Serving size: one bar

- Calories: 190.5 calories
- Fats: 18.53g
- Carbohydrates: 1.5g
- Protein: 4.25g
- Fiber: 2g

What to use

For the bars:

- Erythritol (1 cup)
- Unsalted butter, melted (6 tbsps.)
- Eggs (3)
- Vanilla extract (2 tsp)
- Almond flour (1.5 cups)
- Cinnamon (1 tbsps.)
- Salt (0.25 tsp)
- Baking powder (1 tsp)

For the pecan glaze:

- Unsalted butter, (2 tbsps.)
- Heavy whipping cream (0.25 cups)
- Erythritol (1 tsp)
- Chopped pecans (1 cup)

What to do

1. Heat oven to 350 degrees. Mix 1 cup erythritol and 6 tbsps. melted butter in large mixing bowl.
2. Add eggs, blending until smooth. Set aside.
3. In another bowl blend almond flour, cinnamon, salt, and baking powder.
4. Using a hand blender Add dry ingredients with wet ingredients until smooth.
5. In a greased 8x8 baking dish, pound in batter.
6. Melt 2 tablespoons butter in small pan, making sure to scrape any burnt spots. Add in heavy whipping cream and Erythritol. Whisk until thick.
7. Once whipping mix start to bubble, add pecans and cook for 3-5 minutes.
8. Layer pecans on top of batter.
9. Bake at 350 for 20-25 minutes or until the surface looks dry.

Coconut Raspberry Slices

This recipes makes 12 servings, Serving size: one bar

- Calories: 241.5 calories
- Fats: 22.1g
- Carbohydrates: 3.5g
- Protein: 4.6g
- Fiber: 5.3g

What to use

For biscuit layer:

- Large egg (1)
- Baking soda (0.5 tsp)
- Almond meal (2 cups)
- Room temp butter (1 tbsps.)

For coconut layer:

- Unsweetened, coconut milk, canned (1 cup)
- Powdered erythritol (0.33 cup)
- Vanilla bean powder (1 tsp)
- Coconut oil (0.25 cup)
- Unsweetened desiccated coconut (3 cups)
- Sea salt (1 tsp)

For raspberry layer:

- Water (2 tbsps.)

- Raspberries (1 cup)
- Chia seeds (3 tbsps.)
- Powdered erythritol (1 cup)

For the chocolate layer:

- Dark chocolate (4 oz.)

What to do

1. Heat oven to 350 degrees. Mix all biscuit ingredients.
2. Evenly press biscuit mix into a parchment lined 8x8 pan or brownie dish. Bake 15 minutes, they should look lightly browned. Cool.
3. Mix coconut oil and coconut milk over medium-high heat.
4. Mix all coconut layer ingredients together. Combine coconut milk and coconut oil to the mix.
5. Pour coconut mix over biscuit layer in pan and place in freezer to set, about 1 hour.
6. Mix all ingredients for raspberry layer.
7. Once coconut has set, pour raspberries over, place in freezer and set, another hour.
8. Microwave chocolate for 3 minutes or until melted, and pour over set raspberries, place back in freezer for 30 minutes.
9. Remove, cut into about 20 slices and serve, refrigerate leftovers.

Peanut Butter Blocks

This recipe can be prepared within 10 mins.

- Calories: 170 calories
- Fat: 16g
- Protein: 3g
- Sugars: 6g
- Carbohydrates: 9g
- Fiber: 2g

What to use

For the bars:

- Vanilla extract (0.5 tsp)
- Butter (4 oz.)
- Swerve brand Icing sugar style (0.25 cup)
- Peanut butter (0.5 cup)
- Almond flour (0.75 cup)

For the topping:

- Sugar-free chocolate chips (0.5 cup)

What to do

1. Mix all the ingredients and spread into a small 6-inch pan.
2. Melt chocolate chips in microwave 30 seconds.
3. Spread chocolate on top.
4. Refrigerate at least one hour, for better results refrigerate longer.

Conclusion

Thank you for making it to the end of this book. We hope it was informative and able to provide you with all of the tools you need to achieve your goals on the Ketogenic Diet. Now you should be well on your way to starting a keto lifestyle. We hope that even the most novice dieter should be able to walk away after reading this book and feel confident about starting a keto diet.

We learned that cutting carbohydrates removes glucose as the normal source of energy for the body. By doing this, it is forced to start burning fats instead to use as energy. This puts the body into a fasting state called ketosis, and fat loss begins; thus causing weight loss.

Some of the health benefits we discussed included increased memory and strength, healthier digestion, weight loss, diabetic control, and heart health. We also discussed how studies have shown that low-carb and high-protein diets are more favorable than a diet calling for counting calories because people have a more structured outline of what they can and cannot eat.

Lastly, we provided a complete 30-day meal guide as

well as the recipes you need to follow the plan, making your first month on the diet easy as possible.

The next step is to go out there and start your ketogenic diet and begin living a healthier you.

Finally, if you found this book useful in any way, a review on Amazon is always appreciated!

Recipes Index In Alphabetical Order

Arugula Salad with Prosciutto, Parmesan and Fried Eggs............70

Asparagus Egg and Bacon Salad with Dijon Vinaigrette...............93

Bacon Parmesan Spaghetti Squash...88

BLT Lettuce Wraps...87

Braised Cubed Steak with Peppers and Olives Recipe...............148

Broccoli and Cheese Mini Egg Omelets..73

Brussels Sprouts with Crumbled Blue Cheese...........................144

Burger Bites...121

California Spicy Crab Stuffed Avocado......................................120

Cheeseburger Salad...134

Chicken and Cilantro Salad...96

Chicken Pesto Bake...124

Chicken Salad with Strawberries and Spinach.............................84

Chicken Thighs with Artichoke Hearts and Feta Cheese............125

Chicken with Bacon and Green Beans..136

Chicken with Dijon and Lime..155

Chicken with Mushrooms with Garlic White Wine Sauce..........149

Chicken with Tomatoes and Rosemary...82

Cinnamon Pecan Bars..164

Cobb Salad...91

Coconut Chocolate Chip Cookies....................160

Coconut Milk Shrimp with Tomatoes and Cilantro....................151

Coconut Raspberry Slices....................166

Crab Cauliflower Fried Rice....................101

Eggs with Scallions and Tomatoes....................72

Enchilada Chicken Rolls....................130

Flourless Keto Brownies....................158

Garlic and Lime Pork Chops....................145

Garlic Cuban Pork....................103

Grilled Chicken Bruschetta....................132

Grilled Chicken with Spinach and Melted Mozzarella....................156

Grilled Flank Steak with Chimichurri....................153

Grilled Garlic Chicken with Vegetables....................116

Grilled Mediterranean Cedar Plank Salmon....................146

Grilled Prosciutto Wrapped Asparagus....................127

Grilled Salmon Kebabs....................142

Grilled Salmon with Avocado Bruschetta....................107

Grilled Steak Lettuce Tacos....................138

Grilled Steak with Tomatoes, Red Onion and Balsamic....................112

Grilled Tuna Arugula Salad with Lemon Vinaigrette....................81

Guacamole Deviled Eggs....................79

Keto Pound Cake....162

Loaded Baked Omelet Muffins....68

Mini Bell Pepper Loaded Turkey Nachos....128

Onion, Red Pepper and Zucchini Frittata....75

Pancetta with Brussels Sprouts....90

Parmesan Chicken with Broccoli....114

Peanut Butter Blocks....168

Philly Cheesesteak with Portobello Mushrooms....122

Sausage Stuffed Zucchini with Mozzarella Cheese....140

Sautéed Collard Greens with Bacon....78

Sheet Pan Shrimp with Broccolini and Tomatoes....118

Spinach, Feta, and Artichoke Breakfast Bake....66

Steak Kebabs with Chimichurri....105

Tuna Lettuce Wrap With Avocado Yogurt Dressing....94

Turkey Enchilada Stuffed Poblanos....109

Veggie Ham Egg and Cheese Bake....76

Zesty Shrimp and Avocado Salad....98

Zucchini Carpaccio....86

Zucchini Rolls....99

Other Books By Elizabeth Wells

Keto Diet For Beginners
Complete Beginner's Guide To Lose Weight Fast And Live Healthier With Ketogenic Cooking

Would you like to lose weight and feel better without only eating salads? Have you already followed countless diets, without actually seeing any results? This one is different, and the results will speak for themselves.

The Ketogenic Diet, or Keto Diet, is a solid dieting program created back in 1924 by Dr. Russel Wilder and supported by many scientific studies. The Keto Diet is not another diet that promises you everything and delivers you little to nothing! This dieting style lost popularity when some sketchy "lose weight effortlessly" diets came out some years ago, but it is now being acclaimed worldwide again, with famous people following it and new scientific studies being published.

The Keto Diet is based on this principle: your body usually gets energy from the carbs you eat and stores all the excess fats (think about love handles or belly fat). Most diets tell you to stop eating fats to lose weight, however there's a better way to do it.

Some types of fats are healthy and eating them more, while also reducing your intake of carbs, will help you lose weight faster. In fact, if you start eating low carb and high fat your body will use the fats instead of the carbohydrates to produce energy, without actually storing them.

This way, your body will naturally burn fats for you, just by eating the right foods. And the best part is ketogenic foods actually taste really good. Imagine how ketogenic cooking will improve your shape and overall health.

"Once you have been on the ketogenic diet for a few weeks and begun to experience its benefits you will never want to go back to high-carb eating. After all, ketosis is the body's natural state. It's how we were designed to live."

Following this diet is easy when you have the right help. That's why this book will teach you **everything**

you need to know about the keto diet to help you lose weight fast and feel better, without being too tricky or complicated. You'll learn exactly what to eat, what to avoid, what recipes to cook, what to store in your pantry to follow the keto diet correctly and start improving your health right now.

Some benefits you'll get by going keto:

- Lose Weight Fast And In A Natural Way
- Feel Better, Both Mentally And Physically
- Eat Healthy Foods That Actually Taste Good
- Have A Healthy, Younger Looking Skin
- Feel Full Of Energy All Day Long
- Lower Your Triglyceride Levels To Prevent Heart Attacks
- Eat Foods That Won't Leave You Hungry All Day
- Improve Your Physical Performance
- Lower Your Cancer Risk
- And Much, Much More

In this book you'll learn:

- What Is The Ketogenic Diet and How It Works
- All The Real Benefits Of The Ketogenic Diet
- A Complete 14-day Keto Meal Plan To Successfully Go Keto
- 20+ Delicious Keto Recipes For Breakfast, Lunch And Dinner
- A List Of Keto Friendly Foods To Store In Your Pantry
- The Complete Keto Shopping List To Fill Your Cart With Healthy Foods
- How To Know If You Shouldn't Follow This Diet

- Simple Tips And Tricks To Stay Keto While Travelling
- How To Stay On The Keto Diet Through The Holidays
- And Much More

Start improving your health today!

"Keto Diet For Beginners" by Elizabeth Wells is available at Amazon.

Keto Pressure Cooker
101 Delicious Ketogenic Recipes For The Electric Pressure Cooker To Lose Weight Fast And Live Healthier

If you love the ketogenic diet and would like to cook dishes using your electric pressure cooker this book is for you. Cooking keto using an electric pressure cooker will help you save time and money without losing the countless benefits of a high fat, low carb diet.

In this cookbook, you'll find 101 mouthwatering ketogenic recipes for every meal time, breakfast, lunch, dinner, sides and desserts. All the recipes include comprehensive instructions and nutritional values, allowing you to know the amount of calories, fats, carbohydrates and proteins contained in each dish.

With the help of these recipes you will easily transition toward a healthier lifestyle.

Some recipes you'll find:

- Korean Steamed Eggs
- Ham And Pepper Fritatta
- Italian Sausage Kale Soup
- Creamy Cauliflower Chowder
- Cream Of Mushroom
- Shredded Chicken
- Green Beans And Bacon
- Prosciutto Wrapped-asparagus
- Coconut Milk Shrimp
- Salmon With Orange Ginger Sauce
- Garlic Cuban Pork
- Garlic And Parmesan Asparagus
- Pumpkin Cheesecake
- Chocolate Mousse
- Coconut Almond Cake
- Chocolate Cheesecake
- And Much More

Enjoy these keto dishes today!

"Keto Pressure Cooker" by Elizabeth Wells is available at Amazon.

Keto Slow Cooker
101 Delicious Ketogenic Recipes For The Slow Cooker To Lose Weight Fast And Live Healthier

Are you on a ketogenic diet and would love to cook using your slow cooker? Imagine putting a bunch of ingredients in your slow cooker before going to work and coming home to a delicious keto approved meal.

In this cookbook, you'll find 101 delicious ketogenic recipes you can easily cook with your slow cooker. Just follow the simple steps, put all the ingredients in, and let the slow cooker do the rest. You'll discover recipes for chilis, soups, stews, beef meals, poultry and pork dishes, desserts and other tasty treats that will help you save time without losing the countless benefits of a high fat, low carb diet.

All the recipes include step-by-step instructions and nutritional values, allowing you to know the amount of calories, fats, carbohydrates and proteins contained in each dish. And remember, you don't have to spend your entire day in the kitchen to cook healthy dishes.

Some recipes you'll find:

- Chicken Chorizo Soup
- Hare Stew
- BBQ Pulled Beef
- Balsamic Chicken Thighs
- Cuban Ropa Vieja
- Cranberry Pork Roast
- Poached Salmon
- Zucchini Bread
- Chile Verde
- Summertime Veggies
- Jamaican Jerk Roast
- Raspberry Coconut Cake
- Lemon Frosted Cake
- Grain-Free Granola
- And Much More

Enjoy your new recipes today!

"Keto Slow Cooker" by Elizabeth Wells is available at Amazon.

Keto Diet

Complete Beginner's Guide To Lose Weight Fast And Live Healthier With Ketogenic Cooking

Have you already tried every known diet without seeing any results? Are you willing to lose weight and improve your health but don't want to quit eating some of your loved dishes?

You've come to the right place. The Ketogenic Diet is a popular dieting program that has been around for decades. The Keto Diet is not another fad regime that promises you everything and delivers you little to nothing! This dieting style has been created by Dr. Russell Wilder back in 1924 and is proven and supported by many scientific studies. It lost popularity when some fad “lose weight quick” diets came out some decades ago.

Recently it is being rediscovered and is already acclaimed worldwide. The Keto Diet is well known for being a low carb diet, where the body produces ketones instead of glucose to be used as energy. This will help it burn fats to produce energy without storing them and will drastically reduce the amount of weight you accumulate.

"Eating high fat and low carb offers many health, weight loss, physical and mental performance benefits."

You don’t have to quit eating fats to lose weight. You’ll still be able to enjoy food that actually tastes good and makes you happy.

In this book you’ll learn how the Keto Diet works and how you can start improving your health right now by cooking delicious dishes.

These are some of the benefits you’ll get:

- Lose weight naturally and easily
- Feel well, both mentally and physically
- Keep your skin younger looking
- Eat healthy foods you actually like
- Satisfy your appetite without remaining hungry all day
- Achieve a lower blood pressure
- Prevent heart attacks by lowering your triglyceride levels
- Increase your energy and improve your physical performance
- Lower your cancer risk

- And much more

Following this diet without any help can be complex, especially if you're a beginner. That's why this book aims to teach you everything you need to know to improve your eating habits and your life, without being too tricky or complicated.

In this book you'll learn:

- What is the Ketogenic Diet
- What You Should Eat (And What You Shouldn't)
- 43 Recommended Foods (with calories, grams of carbs, proteins and fats contained)
- How To Follow The Keto Diet Correctly (Most People Get This Wrong)
- 3 Signs That You've Reached Ketosis
- The Benefits Of Going Keto
- 50 Quick And Easy To Cook Keto Recipes
- And much more

What are you waiting for? Start eating healthier today!

"Keto Diet" by Elizabeth Wells is available at Amazon.

Ketogenic Diet Guide For Beginners:

"Ketogenic Diet Guide For Beginners" by Elizabeth Wells is available at Amazon.

Printed in Great Britain
by Amazon